Moving Beyond Survival - The Early Years

How We Thrive With Autism

Tracie Wolf

First edition 2023

Book Cover by Tracie Wolf

Excerpt from "Welcome to Holland" by Emily Perl Kingsley. Used with permission of the author Copyright 1987

ISBN: 979-8-9887541-1-4 (paperback)

ISBN: 979-8-9887541-0-7 (e-book)

Dedication

For my husband, because you love me so much you never tell me "No!"

And

For my son, for the gift of your permission to share our life experiences so they may help others thrive in the world that is autism.

I love you both more than I can ever express in words.

And

For my editors, Alicia, Anthony, Crystal, and Melissa. Thank you for volunteering to help make this project as professional and thought-provoking as possible. I absolutely couldn't have done it without you!

Contents

Introduction   1

1. Welcome To A Whole New Way of Looking at Life!   9

2. Our First Two Years   17

3. The World of Early Intervention   27

4. The First Year of Preschool   47

5. The Eating Program Adventure   59

6. The Second and Third Years of Preschool   69

7. Kindergarten   77

8. The IEP Or The 504   89

9. Your Marriage - Holding Things Together   97

10. Keeping Your Sense of Humor and Joy   107

11. Farewell For Now   115

References   117

Introduction

Someone calls me Mommy, or these days just Mom. It's our 20-year-old son, and he has Autism Spectrum Disorder (ASD). At least that's the current terminology. His initial diagnosis was Asperger Syndrome. In 2002, when he was born, Asperger Syndrome was considered a different diagnosis, separate from autism. Then, in 2013, the diagnosis terminology changed again. The biggest change regarding diagnosis was that four separate disorders (Autistic Disorder, Asperger Syndrome, Pervasive Developmental Disorder Not Otherwise Specified, and Disintegrative Disorder) would now be grouped under the diagnosis of Autism Spectrum Disorder.

A clinical report from January 2020 in the publication, Pediatrics, by Dr. Susan L. Hyman, provides a detailed history and description of Autism Spectrum Disorder and discusses diagnosis, signs, and more. It's a long article, but if you are looking for information, it's a good place to start.

Our physician explained to us ASD is considered a huge umbrella. The closer you get to the center of the umbrella, the more severe the symptoms. Toward the edge of the umbrella is Asperger's Syndrome, which is considered high functioning with less severe symptoms.

This flexibility and continued evolution in diagnosis terminology are indicative of the medical community's difficulty in diagnosing autism. It also reflects society's ambition to understand autism better.

No two ASD individuals are exactly alike. Just as neurotypical individuals do, they have their own separate identities and difficulties. For lack of a better term, our son is considered "high functioning," but he didn't just pop out that way. It took years of patience and diligent work on his part and mine to get to where we are today.

I was clueless when the word autism first appeared on my computer. It never occurred to me, as a first-time mother, that the behavior our child was exhibiting was not typical. Considering the risks of having a child at a more advanced age (35 and up at the time), autism wasn't mentioned as a possibility. Upon hearing the potential diagnosis, my search for information began. It was difficult back then to find facts and guidance that were relatable and easy to understand. My search on the Internet revealed medical research papers beyond my ability to comprehend. Overwhelmed and undereducated, my experience as a legal secretary was not going to help with understanding advanced terminology from a medical perspective.

As the years went by and we finally were able to get a diagnosis, there was still a depressing lack of self-help books for the average parent looking for advice on raising children with autism, specifically high-functioning children. Today, there is a myriad of information available for parents on the Internet: countless organizations, self-published books, and blogs with information at your fingertips. It can still feel incredibly overwhelming.

Why A Book?

What a lovely thought a blog would have been, but I barely had time to sleep! Even without a blog, people often would expound on how we should handle a situation with or without asking for their opinions. While listening respectfully is important and part of my personality, arguing with people who think they "know it all" is not worth my time. Sometimes, their advice can be helpful. Other times, it's worth a smile and a "thank you for your point of view." A blog would have only added stress to my already stressful life.

When our son began his teenage years, my time freed up a bit. While these years were still stressful, they did not fill so much of my schedule. Writing a book about all our successes and struggles living with autism as a family was my choice. However, it was important that both our son and my husband approved of publicly placing our personal life on display. You wouldn't be reading this now if they had not given me their consent. In fact, I still check regularly with our autistic son to make sure that he is still ok with my writing and having a podcast about our life experiences. Each time he assures me that it is fine.

My goal was to write something short and easy to read because parents don't have time for much more. As parents, we are consumed by advocating, teaching, and nourishing our children. We do this all while not getting enough sleep or eating regular and healthy meals. Our time is precious, and it is my hope that by making this book an easy read, parents will have time to dive in and enjoy it while they learn.

After a good portion of the first draft was written, a close friend pushed me into separating the one book into three. She had a valid point. No one starting this journey wants to read about the high school experiences of an autistic teenager. Likewise, a parent of an autistic teenager may not want to read about our son's preschool experiences. We as a community want information that is relevant to what stage we are now experiencing. It was great advice!

This is the first book in a three-part series. It focuses on birth through Kindergarten. The next book will focus on Grades 1 through 12 and also includes a chapter on our son's experience with virtual learning caused by the COVID-19 pandemic. The final book will be about our son's transition into early adulthood.

Difficulties with "High-Functioning" Autism

"High functioning" are the keywords that make it so very difficult for us to find help as parents. Although this term has fallen out of favor in the autism community of late, it is the term that was used often while our son was growing up. The fact that our children may seem to function or "mask" quite well makes it easy for them to fall through the cracks, especially once they are in a school environment. If you do not spend a lot of time with our son, you would never even know that he has autism. When he was younger it was more obvious. It's been my experience that when symptomology is not severe or obvious, we often make excuses or others make them for us. A child like ours can be described as any of the following: quirky, high-spirited, full of energy, introverted and shy, or pushy and strong-willed. As they grow older, they can become so good at mimicking those around them and "masking" their difficulties, that those who do not know them can't tell that there is anything different about them. But there is a difference; and as Mom or Dad, you know it. They struggle because of it. Oh, do they struggle! Countless times we heard, "He may grow out of it." "He may have a learning disability, but let's wait and see how things progress." Or, my favorite line, "He'll eat when he's hungry. He won't starve." No, No. and NO!

Once, a well-known neuropsychologist asked me if we were sure of our son's diagnosis. I smiled and told him to spend an hour with our son. At the end of the hour, he came out and said, "You're right." These children can be very hard to diagnose. Yet, these are the children who, with their parents' love, understanding, and perseverance, along with the help of medical and educational specialists, can grow up to become thriving and mature adults. Hopefully, someday in the not-too-distant future, society will accept these individuals for who they are and not limit them because they may need certain adjustments to live and work with their autism.

Because of how society has treated disabled people in the past, some parents struggle with the "stigma" associated with an autism diagnosis. I never worried about it and was relieved when we finally received an official diagnosis. It opened up a whole new world of services and help for our son. We received speech therapy, occupational therapy, and many other services (most of the time for free or covered by insurance) because we had that official diagnosis. There is no stigma associated with someone having a disability, only doors that can open to aid that person. Sometimes those doors may seem to be stuck. It's okay. This book will discuss successful ways we pushed those doors open when we needed to do so.

There are those that argue with me that their child will be treated differently. Guess what? Your child IS different. Not less, but different. Whether or not you have a diagnosis will not change how they are treated by others. Never once have we regretted getting a diagnosis. You won't either.

If you have picked up this book, well done, and thanks! Some parents bury their heads in the sand hoping "nothing is wrong." Others feel so overwhelmed that they become paralyzed with fear of the future, unable to see beyond the "awful news" to the beautiful gift that they have been given. A handful of parents can never get past the "why" this happened and some focus only on finding a "cure." For a sad few, anger over the circumstances they now face interferes with developing a future full of success for their child.

You have taken an important step toward helping your child be successful in life just by acknowledging there is a difference and reaching out for guidance and help. Keep it up. You are on the right path.

One Day At A Time And This Book

Raising an autistic child taught me the value of taking one day at a time. Before we had our son, my life was planned. These plans were set for weeks, even years into the future. In order to maintain my sanity, I had to adjust my thinking about life and the future after he was born.

Every day is a fresh start. Yesterday was really hard but you have another chance today to try something else that may make it less hard. Each day builds upon the next. You grow. Your child grows. No one knows what the future will hold and time does not stop. Let your fears of the future go for now if you are worried about it. Your child will develop at their own pace. When you get to the future, you will have had enough experience that you will know how to request help for the next phase of your child's life. You will help your child thrive one day at a time. It is not advantageous to dwell on all the things that can go wrong in the future. After all, doesn't every parent worry about their child? Development and improvement will occur over time.

Many times parents have come to me to express their frustration or ask for advice. I have sought advice from more experienced parents as well. In 2004, there were few organized sources of information when researching autism. A few years ago, thinking about the advice given and received, I made the decision to write this book. Personal experience is priceless. Sharing our story with others gives them hope for their future, ideas on how to succeed, and helps them realize they are not alone in their struggles.

Personal experience and how people dealt with difficulty can be found in blogs, of course. But this book combines in one place all the experiences we as a family had in raising our autistic son thus far in a readily available and easily relatable format. This story is written by a parent who raised an average autistic child, for parents who are trying to do the same thing.

It contains practical experiences that worked for us as we raised our son. It can and should stimulate you to think differently about autism. It will help you break through that mental box we often place ourselves in when faced with a difficult situation.

Links to sources for further information are provided at the back of the book. You are not going to find a lot of medical information in this book. When you have medical questions, please talk to a physician or therapist about them. If they can't answer your questions, seem disinterested, or make you feel stupid, then look for another medical provider. As the saying goes, there are no dumb questions, only unanswered ones!

Opinions based on my own experiences aren't wrong or right. They are just opinions. My hope is that this book helps you feel less alone and offers you avenues that you may not have thought to try, but please do not take my opinions as fact. Do your own research and draw your own conclusions about what works for you and your child.

Also, please do not compare our child to yours. I can't emphasize this enough. Every child develops differently in their own time. You will learn and know what is right for them. In time, you will begin to see your own child's successful path. Of course, you should listen to your physicians, therapists, and educational specialists. But if your son or daughter is struggling with a milestone, be patient and resist the urge to compare them to others. Ask for more advice if you need it. Take a deep breath and trust that it will happen eventually with patience and perseverance. It will!

The final and most important reason for writing these books is our son. Someday, perhaps he will find a significant other and become a father. However, if that doesn't work for him, there is no judgment on that decision. If he has an autistic child, giving him our story in writing as a guide to help him understand his early journey from a parent's perspective is invaluable. It will provide him with knowledge of what we did to help him thrive. He does not remember most of his early years.

As mentioned before, we had many conversations with our son about this book during its creation. His permission for me to share his life story was my top priority. He believes that his personal struggles and successes can help others who may be experiencing the same thing.

Our journey is not the "end of the world." It's just a different version of the parenthood journey. This book and the ones that follow will share our journey. If the experiences shared and the information provided helps, then the time it took to write this book was well spent.

Keep reading, researching, and reaching out. *No one else will do this for your child.* You are your child's greatest advocate until they learn to advocate for themselves (which you will also teach them). It's up to you to help your child move beyond survival mode and to thrive in a life that suits them. Ditch the worry. You've got this!

Chapter 1

Welcome To A Whole New Way of Looking at Life!

I am often asked to describe the experience of raising a child with a disability - to try to help people who have not shared that unique experience to understand it, to imagine how it would feel. It's like this......

When you're going to have a baby, it's like planning a fabulous vacation trip - to Italy. You buy a bunch of guide books and make your wonderful plans. The Coliseum. The

Michelangelo David. The gondolas in Venice. You may learn some handy phrases in Italian. It's all very exciting.

After months of eager anticipation, the day finally arrives. You pack your bags and off you go. Several hours later, the plane lands. The flight attendant comes in and says, "Welcome to Holland."

"Holland?!?" you say. "What do you mean Holland?? I signed up for Italy! I'm supposed to be in Italy. All my life I've dreamed of going to Italy."

But there's been a change in the flight plan. They've landed in Holland and there you must stay.

The important thing is that they haven't taken you to a horrible, disgusting, filthy place, full of pestilence, famine and disease. It's just a different place.

So you must go out and buy new guide books. And you must learn a whole new language. And you will meet a whole new group of people you would never have met.

It's just a different place. It's slower-paced than Italy, less flashy than Italy. But after you've been there for a while and you catch your breath, you look around.... and you begin to notice that Holland has windmills....and Holland has tulips. Holland even has Rembrandts.

But everyone you know is busy coming and going from Italy... and they're all bragging about what a wonderful time they had there. And for the rest of your life, you will say "Yes, that's where I was supposed to go. That's what I had planned."

And the pain of that will never, ever, ever, ever go away ... because the loss of that dream is a very very significant loss.

But... if you spend your life mourning the fact that you didn't get to Italy, you may never be free to enjoy the very special, the very lovely things ... about Holland.

Every few years, this comes up on my Facebook page as a "memory," and sharing it again with friends and family is a true joy. Sharing this the last time on Facebook, another friend posted, "Love this, and 'Holland' is remarkable!" She said this because our sons grew up together, and she personally witnessed many of the difficulties he conquered in his early years. What a lovely comment; and, yes, I believe our son is remarkable as well. "Welcome to Holland" makes me think,

"Yes! That's it!" For me, nothing better encapsulates the feeling of finding out that your child has autism.

So, welcome to the parenthood path of autism! You are going to change and grow as a parent more than you can possibly imagine. Get ready for an amazing journey of learning about yourself, your significant other, and – most of all - your child.

Recognize that your vision of being a parent will totally change. If it hasn't yet, it's about to. "Welcome to Holland" screams, "This is not what I signed up for!" The sense of bewilderment and yes, anger, that we as parents of a child with autism (special needs) experience comes through loud and clear. Ms. Kingsley expresses our sense of grief. You feel her understanding as she talks about the loss of all her dreams and expectations. Most importantly, her story speaks of not missing out on how awesome your journey will be if you just focus on enjoying the experience with your child. She does all this using the metaphor of traveling to a different county. It's genius!

Once you have read it, take a few minutes to digest it. One of the emotions spoken about is anger. Anger visits me often. It simmers, goes away for a while, and then something will happen. Wham! It's back.

If you experience this anger as well, do not be ashamed. Yes, you are angry! It is okay as long as you resist the temptation to get bogged down in that anger and wallow in it. It is not your child's fault that your dreams and expectations about their life do not match with their reality. Some people get obsessed with the "why" this happened. As a parent, it's more important to deal with what is happening in the moment. Personally, the why is less important to me than how we move forward toward the future. We can't change the past and can only deal with each day, one day at a time.

The CDC has a webpage on the debated causes of autism. I'm not going to go into them. However, you need to get past this stage to help your child. There is no harm in looking into the "why." Do some careful research (not everything is a trusted source) and, then, be done with it. *Focusing all your efforts on why this happened will not help you prepare your child for the future.*

If you feel the above story from Kingsley doesn't fit your circumstance, here is another quote from a blog written by Kristen Groseclose. In her blog, she explains that for her the following quote is a more accurate description of what she is going through raising a child with special needs. It reads, *"My barn having burned down, I can see the moon."* - Mizuta Masahide. It's a powerful message in that everything is gone but you can still see the beauty of life.

Finding quotes like these and others along your way as you research your child's needs should tell you one thing. YOU ARE NOT ALONE! You may feel very alone, but you are not. There are others, many others, who have faced or are facing the issues that you are experiencing right now. Never underestimate the power of sitting down and having a chat with a willing partner in this battle to thrive. Search us out. Find a support group and make the time to go in person if possible. Listen to podcasts. Search Facebook for "autism groups." We are there for you and our favorite conversation is about how we have endured and triumphed through a particular phase and how we did it. We are an invaluable source of information and support. Do not be shy, we are here for you because someone along our journey was there for us.

How It All Began

My parenthood journey began at the age of thirty when we had already been married for seven years. The Catholic priest conducting our interview before our marriage was a bit shocked to hear that we were not sure that we wanted to have children. After a moment of hesitation, the very nice priest asked us, "Well, if God should choose to give you a child, would you love and raise him in the Catholic faith."

Our response was, "Sure;" but, really neither of us had any clue what a very extraordinary child we were going to receive twelve years later.

We went through life with its various challenges. Money was tight for years as we struggled to put my husband through college without putting ourselves severely in debt. Fighting depression, changing jobs numerous times, and seeking therapists and medication to help were a regular part of my life. During those first seven years, never once did the thought of having a child occur to me. Then, turning thirty, an alarm went off. My biological clock kicked in and having a baby became a priority. As I told my husband this, he was flabbergasted; a great word that truly described the open-mouthed astonished look on his face. Two and a half years of discussions finally ended in an agreement that we would try to have a child.

At this point, you are probably asking yourself, "Why is she telling me about her life before her son was born?" Understanding how hard we worked, and how important having a child was to me, will help you appreciate our story a bit more. However, while joking about my biological clock going off, I never want our son (or you) to think there is any regret in having him, despite our difficulties. Being a parent, a mother specifically, has been the most awesomely rewarding experience of my life. Raising our son is my greatest achievement in life. That is probably not going to change. This experience forged me into a new person and helped me understand the meanings of strength, sacrifice, patience, and most of all the human capacity for great love.

Another two and a half years elapsed before we got pregnant (with a little bit of medical help). The agony of wanting to have a child and not being able to conceive is something that really lingers with me, even after all these years. Holding my friends' babies and talking, even with my husband, about having a child was extremely painful. Each unsuccessful month would result in hysterical sobbing, most of the time in the shower so he wouldn't know. Every failed attempt hurt me almost physically. One day in particular, there was considerable crying and yelling at God, "Why won't you let me have a baby? Don't you think I would be a good mother? Why, why, why?!" My heart goes out to those that struggle. I've been there; and, yet, even today, knowing what to say to someone who is facing the same struggle gives me difficulty. For me, the fix was fairly easy. In the end and with some medication and divine intervention, we were given a gift. We were going to have our own bundle of joy.

My pregnancy was relatively routine. Showing almost immediately, the doctor sent me for an ultrasound, just in case. My numbers were indicative of a single fetus, but my tummy had really popped out. They found placenta previa, but otherwise a normal growing fetus. We opted for amniocentesis to rule out chromosome-related issues. That was a difficult decision to make. The idea of amniocentesis scared me, but my husband was adamant. He worked just as hard to make this baby, so we had the procedure. The test results came out "normal," and they told us that the placenta had moved up and out of the birth canal as the baby had grown. This was excellent news.

Changing my OBGYN at around six months was necessary. A good friend, who was also a medical professional, insisted. I suffered from vertigo and fibroid cysts that were quite painful. She felt I wasn't getting the care that was needed and pushed hard for me to seek another physician. It was an excellent choice. Up until she retired a few years ago, that new doctor was still my OBGYN.

Because of leaking amniotic fluid a week before my actual due date, the decision was made to admit me to the hospital. After another ultrasound, two choices were presented to us. The first choice was to try to deliver the baby vaginally, but the result of that choice most likely would be a very long labor and still may have resulted in having to have a c-section. The other choice was to just have a c-section. My reaction was, "You are giving me a choice? Will others think poorly of me if my choice is to have a c-section and accuse me of taking the easy way out?" How ridiculous was that kind of thinking? In those days, worrying about what other people would think, happened to me often. Conquering this worry as our son grew older was difficult.

As the doctor performed the c-section, she told us we had made the right choice. The baby, although facing the correct direction, had wedged his head in my hip cavity. The umbilical cord was wrapped around his head and over his mouth. A vaginal delivery was not a safe option.

That first cry, incredible! One quick kiss and then they whisked him away. He was on an alarm for his breathing for a day or two because there was still amniotic fluid in the lungs. (A vaginal birth has the added bonus of squeezing the amniotic fluid out.) He was healthy otherwise. Four days later, we got to take him home. My husband and I looked at each other as we drove out of the parking lot and laughed with joy - so strange being allowed to take a baby home. We were ready, or so we thought.

Chapter 2

Our First Two Years

Looking back to that first full year - there were things that I didn't notice about our son's development. His lack of crawling bothered me considerably, but speaking to several people and hearing many stories about how their son or daughter "just got up and walked" helped me feel less anxious. My mother-in-law told me that my husband did the same thing. At eleven months, our son began to walk and that was right on target for development.

I did pay careful attention to childhood milestones, often consulting with a book received from a friend as a baby shower gift. He seemed to be meeting all the milestones up until about a year old. He was a quiet child. We hadn't had a lot of exposure to young children, so the lack of babbling wasn't noticed. We traveled everywhere together, and he was a remarkably easy kid to be around until about twelve months. Then, small things began to trigger my attention. He couldn't speak or interact with his peers, and he couldn't transition from one environment to another. For instance, he could not transition from being asleep to being awake without tears if woken early, if we were leaving the house or an event he would cry and fight with us. Forget going to "Mommy and Me" classes of any kind. I'm jumping ahead, however. Let's start with our first traumatic experience.

A Hospital Admission

At around the two-week mark, we had a problem. The experience was very distressing for us all. Beginning with diarrhea for no apparent reason, he was in so much pain that he would stop feeding to scream and then latch onto the bottle again. After eleven days and numerous doctor visits, we ended up being told we needed to take him to the nearest children's hospital in the city.

It was about five days before Christmas in the middle of a blizzard. The snow was coming down hard, and we were told we couldn't wait. They were terribly sorry to have to send us there in such bad weather, but we had to go immediately. On the way, we watched a tractor-trailer begin to lose control on the highway in front of us. I am absolutely positive that we wouldn't be here today if he hadn't been able to gain control and keep the trailer from jackknifing. That visual is easily pulled from my memory. It still chills me.

Unfortunately, "there was no room at the inn." The hospital rooms were all full. Our first night there was in the playroom, which had been made into an extra room for the overflow. Bright and cheery holiday decorations were everywhere. Christmas music played softly from a boombox. Seeing and hearing all this holiday joy around me was hard. Alone and scared for our son, Christmas was the farthest thing from my mind. When a family showed up to play in our room, I thought, "Are you kidding me?" Hunting down a staff nurse and asking if they were going to continue to allow people to come to play in the room where we were staying was hard. They closed the room down after the group left. I learned a crucial parental lesson that day: voice your questions. Sitting back and assuming people will look out for you and your child is not realistic. Ask your questions calmly and rationally, but do not keep silent when important issues arise.

We told our story over and over again to the doctors. We kept careful notes of everything and gave them very detailed information about what we had gone through for eleven days. This seemed to amaze them for some reason. They took our son off all food and planned to hook him up to an IV. Leaving the room when they drew blood from his feet in the emergency room was a matter of survival for me. When the nurse kindly offered to have me come along for the IV procedure, my response was, "No thank you." As a side note, I have been blessed (or cursed) with an exceptional memory when it comes to events, especially traumatic ones. The nurse, who was initially concerned at my response, completely understood after my explanation. I have no regret in making either of those decisions. Saying "No thank you" was okay; there was no judgment from the nurse. Even if there had been, it was the right decision for me at the time. This is another example of speaking up when it's important to you. I'm a fast learner.

On the second day, they performed an upper and lower GI. They didn't need anesthesia: our son slept through the whole procedure. The diagnosis was a milk protein allergy. We were released after two nights in the hospital. They offered to have us stay another night, but we had been moved to a shared regular room by then. My neighbor was noisy and inconsiderate. The prior night, I had walked the halls for hours with a heavy, crying child in my arms. "Send me home please" was my response.

Once his digestive system settled, we began to introduce him to a formula that "disguised" the milk protein. He accepted the new formula well. However, three months went by before we stopped seeing blood in his stool. It was a very long three months of follow-up visits and assurances that his bowels would take a while to heal.

A year later we were back at the same hospital for our "milk challenge." This allergic "challenge" involved giving him milk and waiting around to see if he had any reaction - all day. Since no reaction was observed, we began to introduce milk back into his diet and watched

him carefully. He was fine and didn't have any trouble drinking
milk from that day forward.

More Issues

As he began to grow, I relished being a mother and loved every
part of it. Motherhood for me had been even better than expected.
The last missing puzzle piece in life had been found. Wholeness
was achieved. Suddenly, happiness was the norm. My depression
miraculously disappeared. I never imagined that one person could
complete me so much.

Our son's stomach and bowels balanced out; but around eight
months, he wouldn't let me feed him with a utensil anymore. He
would eat with his hands but refused to learn how to hold a fork or
spoon. Slowly, he began to refuse food. "Brand-specific" became
very important. He seemed to be able to taste even the slightest
change. It happened so gradually that it did not seem to be a big
problem at first. When he was hungry, he would only eat foods he
considered acceptable; but finding foods that he would eat began
to get harder and harder. By the middle of his second year, his
food choices were very limited. The significance was beyond me. I
buried my head in the sand. For a long time, no one said anything
to me or expressed that this wasn't the norm. However, it is very
typical for an ASD child with sensory issues!

In his early months, he took many short naps throughout the
day. These eventually solidified into one long nap (two hours or more)
in the middle of the day. He didn't transition well to wakefulness
if woken earlier than two hours. Then, night terrors began. Not
knowing what they were, my remedy was rocking and holding him
as he cried and screamed, caught in some terrible nightmare. Often
taking as long as forty-five minutes for him to "wake up" from a nap
or calm down in the middle of the night, there seemed to be no reason

for the problems. His screaming cries were heart-wrenching. This continued all the way through his second year and into his third.

I thought all of these things were just part of the early years of being a mom, right? Sometimes things are not easy, but that's life. Banging his head on the floor - well, that was a bit odd, but I was CLUELESS!

Good Friends

Around eighteen months after our son's birth, some good friends invited me out for dinner. This was not odd, as we would try and schedule a dinner a few times a year to catch up and just celebrate being friends. At the end of the dinner, my friends surrounded me in the parking lot and brought up a topic they had been discussing for three months. At the risk of losing my friendship, they told me as gently as possible that they thought that our son needed to be evaluated by early intervention. They told me to call our pediatrician and get the phone number from their office.

They explained that they suspected that something was wrong with our little boy. They told me that they were not sure exactly what was wrong, but that early intervention could evaluate him and give him services if he needed them. Of course, they knew what the evaluations would show but didn't want to say what they suspected. It still amazes me how worried they were that saying something would make me angry enough with them to end years of friendship. They sympathized with how hard we worked to have a baby and felt horrible. Anger was the farthest thing from my mind. They were all loving beautiful friends, and I still tell them how grateful I am that they chose to "risk our friendship" and speak up about their worries.

When a special education teacher, a nurse, and an occupation-al therapist tell you they think something is wrong with your eigh-teen-month-old, if you're smart, you listen! Having the right frame of mind and being open to their suggestions was really important. Maintaining a balance between *using your voice to speak up and knowing when to listen to good advice* can be difficult. Some people become overly sensitive and refuse to even consider suggestions from family and friends. Others are so busy telling you what they need, they forget that learning to listen is equally as important. The advice received from many different sources over the years helped me be a better parent and caregiver. Speaking up is important, but so is listening.

Frustrated with our son's difficulties and feeling like a failure as his mother, my thoughts were all about the question, "What is wrong with me?" Other friends did not have issues with their children like this. Figuring that there couldn't be any harm in calling early intervention, I reached out to our pediatrician the very next day.

The pediatrician's office put me off, saying "Let's wait until he's at least two years old before we do this." Upon hearing what was said, one of my friends told me to call them back and insist on getting that number. Scheduling an evaluation date and getting that evaluation can take time. If something is wrong, you want the therapy to start sooner rather than later. With very little problem, the pediatrician provided me with the phone number when I called them back. Taking a deep breath, my next call was to early intervention. That one call changed my life and that of our son.

<u>Early Intervention</u>

In New Jersey, sixteen years ago, when you called early intervention, they had a checklist of questions they asked about your child's development. This procedure really has not changed much even after all these years. In the References/Links section of this book, on the NJ.gov site they go over early intervention services available in New Jersey and address "frequently asked questions." I found it when I did an Internet search for my state. The Individuals with Disabilities Education Act (IDEA) requires that early intervention be available in all states. Each state will have its own definition of what constitutes a developmental delay. Parentcenterhub.org has a great website with further explanations and links.

As an example, this is what happens in New Jersey when you seek out early intervention. A service coordinator will talk with you about your concerns and how to obtain referral information. Referrals can come from a number of sources: physicians, hospitals, childcare programs, public health facilities, social services, and, of course, a parent. Then, your permission is gained to perform what they call a "multidisciplinary evaluation/assessment of your child's developmental levels and needs." In this case, multidisciplinary means that they will be evaluating your child in multiple developmental categories or "disciplines." In our state, this evaluation is provided at no cost to the family.

To be eligible for services, a child must meet the criteria in at least one of two categories. The first category is having a developmental delay in two of these areas: physical, cognitive, communication, social or emotional, and/or adaptive areas. They measure the child's placement by comparing it with the general average in a developmental area. They call this the mean. If your child places below the mean by a certain standard or percentage that is pre-set, they will qualify in that area. Your child must qualify in at least two of the above category areas to fall under developmental delay for services.

The second category is called "conditions with high probability." Children in this category already have an identified pre-existing condition that more than likely will cause some developmental delays. To qualify in this category, a written confirmation from a medical provider confirming the diagnosis and the probability of developmental delays is required.

If you qualify after the evaluation, an Individualized Family Service Plan (IFSP) is developed with your child's needs in mind. The plan will describe what services they will be providing. Therapy services can be provided in your home, at a community agency, or in a childcare setting. For us, the most natural environment was our home. An IFSP can include things such as assistive technology, developmental intervention, family training, and more.

Early intervention developmental services revolve around you, the family. They share knowledge and provide positive-based parenting concepts. They can also provide networking opportunities, speech therapy, occupational therapy, physical therapy, and much, much more. The cost of services depends on insurance and family income and size. For our son's services, there was no out-of-pocket expense for us.

When I made the initial call to early intervention, the questions pertaining to development were most alarming. It was like they knew our child intimately and had spent every day of his life with him. Did he do this? Yes. Does he do that? Yes. The questions went on and on, and my answers were always in the affirmative. After the phone call, there was an interesting mix of relief and apprehension. The relief was because someone else already knew about the struggles that we were experiencing on a daily basis. The apprehensive part was for the same reason. How could they know?

The day came for the evaluation. After they "played" with our son and asked more questions, we sat down for their results and recommendations. The exact scene is still in my head: where each of us sat at the kitchen table, where the papers were placed, the light filtering in through the windows indicating the time of day. They felt that our son would benefit from some of their therapy services. Therapy involved a person coming to our house twice a week for a few hours. Depending on our income and health insurance, we might be required to pay a small amount. They believed that our son was experiencing something called Sensory Integration Dysfunction, which can make a child overly sensitive or under-sensitive to certain stimuli. Today, Sensory

Integration Dysfunction is now called Sensory Processing Disorder and is a neurological disorder. Familydoctor.org has a well-written explanation about Sensory Processing Disorder if you are interested in checking it out.

Early intervention also recommended that we call our local children's hospital and have our son medically evaluated as soon as possible by a neurologic team. Requesting an evaluation scheduled at a children's hospital is easy; but depending on the hospital, you probably won't receive an appointment date before six months. Some parents have to wait even longer. As frustrating as it is to have to wait a significant amount of time, make that appointment anyway.

Never once was autism mentioned during our initial meeting with early intervention. They seemed very sad when explaining to us about Sensory Integration Dysfunction. They also were very careful about how they phrased their statements. Their sadness and careful suggestions about their findings, made alarm bells go off in my head. Why were they so unhappy for us? Why did they speak to us so carefully as if the situation was a bomb that needed to be disarmed, one wire at a time? Having never heard of Sensory Integration Dysfunction, at the first opportunity, I fired up my computer and began to do some research. Almost immediately, the word autism appeared in connection with it. Were they saying our son was autistic? Is that why they were so sad and careful? Is there no cure? Is he going to get worse? How did this happen? Oh my God - how do I tell my husband?

For us, the nearest children's hospital required all new patients to ask for an appointment and fill out a form online. As a parent, you were not permitted to speak to anyone initially: they would contact us. We waited and waited and finally were contacted with an appointment date for three months in the future. In the meantime, early intervention therapy began when our son was about twenty-three months old. He would receive occupational therapy two times a week in our home.

Chapter 3
The World of Early Intervention

"Hello, my name is Blue Train. What is your name? Do you want to play with me?"

Children learn through play, and we were told that early intervention therapy is based on play. The therapists would be using a method invented by Dr. Stanley Greenspan. On our first visit, a nice, soft-spoken woman went through what to expect. Our son wanted nothing to do with her. He ran from her and tried to hide. She was unbelievably patient.

So began a year's worth of home visits from complete strangers who would "play" and teach us how to "play" (for the days they couldn't come out). These strangers soon became friends and wonderful sources of supportive information. I would present a behavior issue that we were experiencing. They would not only offer ways to address the behavior but also explained to me WHY the behavior was happening.

That WHY is very important. Many of our son's behaviors resulted from his sensory issues. We were told, if you address the sensory issue, the behavior issue can begin to resolve, perhaps even completely. Time and again, we found this to be true with our son.

It's amazing what you can cope with in a child's behavior if you understand WHY the behavior is happening. Remember the head banging on the floor? That was because our son was seeking a stimulus to self-organize (calm) himself. How to fix this? Jumping and joint compression worked. What about his inability to transition away from an activity? We still couldn't do any organized class without him wandering around, or throwing a complete physical fit when leaving. Now, however, giving him warnings at twenty minutes, ten minutes, five minutes, and two minutes before we were to leave anywhere began to ease the violence of those meltdowns. When the meltdown came (because things do not get fixed overnight), early intervention taught me how to hold him where he would do me the least amount of damage. Leaving an activity holding our screaming child, arms and legs flailing, knowing the WHY of his behavior made things easier and enabled me to deal with him patiently and calmly. He was not a bad kid. I was not a bad mom. He simply could not transition easily from one event to another. Eventually, he would learn to transition through experience and with my guidance.

Now, I'm not an angel. There were days when, unfortunately, my outlet was screaming at him in frustration. Sometimes crying in the car or crying all the way home was my only other option, because I was so embarrassed, angry, and upset. He witnessed that. However, I do think that knowing WHY he did what he did kept me sane.

Oh, the embarrassment! That was a hard lesson for me to learn. My parents raised me to always be cognizant of what other people think of me. Do not under any circumstances embarrass yourself or your parents! Many years went by before I got over being embarrassed because our son exhibited a particular undesirable behavior. You may not have a problem with feeling this way; and if so, that's good. But, if you are more like me, remind yourself to stop feeling embarrassed. This may be hard for you to accept given how some people may judge you based on your child's behavior. However, you are not going to change that. Someone once told me about a woman who printed up business cards that explained that her child had autism, etc. If that made her feel better, she succeeded in her own way. For me though, all I needed was to have a little talk with myself each time. Some people can't understand. Some people refuse to understand. You can't change that, and it's ultimately not your problem. This self-talk became a mantra for me. For your sake and that of your child, learn to let go of your worry about the judgemental attitude of others. Those people who judge you or your child are not important. They have no idea what you experience on a daily basis. What IS important is that you love your child and are working on helping them learn and grow. You are there for them: that is what should be your focus when those feelings of embarrassment creep in.

Sometimes anger goes hand-in-hand with your embarrassment. You are human; and do not be surprised that during a difficult situation, you become upset when you are being criticized by a stranger or even a fellow family member. If that person is interested in listening to why your child is acting the way they are, feel free to let them know. If they're not interested, it's acceptable to feel free to tell them to mind their own business! Please, however, do not take your anger out on your child. It's not their fault they are acting this way in the early stages of their life.

What do you do when you get home and you are still angry? Your child is happy being back in their home environment. They have forgotten all about the terribly embarrassing way they behaved or didn't even realize they did anything "wrong." Here are a few things to blow off that steam that has built up inside you. I'm speaking from experience.

- Once your child is settled, go into the bedroom, close the door, and scream as loud as you can into your pillow as many times as you need to. When arguing wasn't an option with our son anymore because of my anger, I would lock myself in the bathroom for a few minutes. He would pound on the door telling me to come out. Giggling my response would be, "In a bit." This was perfectly acceptable and kept me from losing my cool and acting in an unproductive way with my child.

- Laughter is fantastic for relieving anger and stress. Pull out your phone and find videos that make you laugh. Do not wait until you need them - look for them early and have them saved for when you will need the boost.

- Crying is also a viable option. Early on, guilt consumed me if my child saw me cry. This felt like weakness because "the parent should be in charge at all times." "The parent does not show weakness." *Parents are still human.* If your child sees you cry, that is okay. Still, if you do not want them to see you cry, that's acceptable too. There were many times I grabbed one of his bigger stuffed animals and sat, rocking back and forth, crying my heart out. I chose to do it where he couldn't see me. If you cope with the anger by crying, remember that there is no shame in it. What works for you is all that matters.

- Finally, if you feel things are just not improving and nothing seems to work for you, seek outside help. Is there a trusted, non-judgmental friend you can call to vent to or, better yet, who will visit and give you a break so you can take a walk? I didn't have anyone to give me a break at a moment's notice. But if you do, use them! If you are like me and do not have someone at hand, perhaps you can reach out for some counseling. Counselors are terrific for teaching us ways to cope with anger and stress. They can remind us of ways to cope we may have forgotten or suggest new coping mechanisms. They push us out of the restrictive mental box we often find ourselves inhabiting during stressful times.

The early intervention therapist didn't just teach us about why a behavior was happening: she also demonstrated therapies to assist with overcoming the sensory issues. Discussing all the activities and therapies we worked on during their year with our son would constitute a whole book all by itself. There were so many! Here are some of my favorites so that you will feel less intimidated if you are apprehensive about reaching out to them.

Deep Pressure

Joint Compression. The name sounds frightening and difficult. It's not, and our son totally thrived on it. We called joint compression "squishes;" and although we started with a regimen many times a day as part of our "sensory diet," the practice eventually became something we did every night at bedtime as part of our routine for MANY years.

The theory behind joint compression is that deep pressure helps a child "organize" their thoughts and calm their emotions - thus the reason we made "squishes" a routine every night before bed. More explanation on joint compression can be found on the website created by North Valley Pediatric Therapy. The authors define in detail what joint compression is and suggest the best times to perform the sensory therapy with your child. In addition, if you are curious to see how it is done there are many YouTube videos to view online demonstrating the therapy.

We started out slowly. He would only let me do "squishes" one or two times. Instead of "tickles," we had a game each night based on the compressions. Eventually, we built up to two sets of ten "squishes" on both arms and legs every night at bedtime. As he grew older, we counted in Spanish for more fun. When Spanish got boring, we switched to French. (You can find out how to count to ten in a foreign language by searching the Internet - a little parental homework that combines therapy with some fun learning for your child.)

We had "squishes" for years and finally stopped when the need for this technique lessened. When he got older, we gave him the choice, every night. "Do you want squishes?" Some nights the answer would be, "Yes," and other nights, "No," until, eventually, the need for the practice faded away. Good thing too! By then my hands couldn't get around parts of his legs to get an effective compression. Yes, you heard me right - We practiced this for years!

Joint compression is not the only way to give deep pressure. Our son was constantly seeking this, so early intervention taught us many ways to provide him with what he needed. When he was a baby, he loved to be swaddled tightly. No unwrapping or arms flying - I used to call him my burrito baby! This did not change as he grew older. We had a game where a blanket was spread on the floor. He would lay on the blanket with his head out. Then we would roll him up with only his head sticking out. His arms were at his side. Nothing poked out but his head and sometimes his feet. Then, just a gentle bit of downward pressure was applied on his legs and arms. He loved it. Now if your child totally freaks if you try this with them, obviously this would not be a therapy that would be good for them. For us, though, blanket wrapping was one of our many favorites and helped him calm.

We also provided some deep pressure by squishing him on the couch. I had him sit on the couch and then would sit between his legs and lay back on him pretending to be unaware he was there. This would make him laugh and laugh. It was fun for both of us. Amazingly, once we were done, he could focus and concentrate enough to work on harder therapies or complete a task for me.

Another type of therapy is called *brushing*- this is often called the Wilbarger Protocol. A good explanation of brushing can be found on the webpage from PlayWorks Therapy, Inc. We purchased a little white plastic brush with soft bristles. However, when we tried this therapy with our son; instead of calming him, brushing seemed to agitate him. Every child on the spectrum is different: what works for one may not work for another, and this is a prime example of that divergence. Do not give up if one particular therapy doesn't seem to work. Try another! The best experience with our early intervention professionals was that they seemed to have an unlimited supply of ideas on different types of therapies. We would describe a problem we were having, and they would explain to us what our child was seeking and suggest a therapy to help with it.

For example, swinging is a therapy. *Swinging and Sensory Integration: How It Works* explains that, "Swinging allows a child to neutralize the disruptions that are caused by their vestibular system,..." What is a vestibular system? It consists of inner ear organs that primarily are "...responsible for how our body and brain react to gravity and objects within our periphery."

Haven't got a swing in your backyard handy? No problem. A sheet or blanket and two people works just as well. Have the child lie down on a blanket then you and a partner pick up the ends and gently swing. The blanket lightly compresses the child's body. Our son loved it! A hammock is great for this as well and you don't need another person to swing your child in one.

We would combine swinging with something he didn't tolerate well; singing! We sang nursery rhymes. He learned to tolerate the singing because he was doing something else that he enjoyed at the same time. Do you know how much singing and music there is in preschool? This was important!

Several other favorite therapies our son enjoyed were "airplane" and "horsey rides." You may remember your parents or family members doing these with you when you were a child. For "airplane" rides, lay on your back and pull your knees to your chest. Have your child gently rest his chest on your knees while holding onto his/her hands. Slowly lift your feet and lower legs to bring your child off the floor. He's flying! We had a therapist who used horsey rides on her back to relax our child. She would carry him on her back around the house as he held onto her neck laughing and giggling the whole time. She would bounce like a horse to give him that jumping feeling. Good stuff!

Jumping is also an excellent therapy for calming and helping your child think more clearly. A friend gave us their mini trampoline after their child grew out of it. It was in our living room for a year and then went out in the garage for outdoor play. Every school day before he would pick up the bus to school, I would have him jump on the mini trampoline while we waited. We kept it in our garage so it stayed clean and bug-free. What if you do not have the funds to buy a mini trampoline and can't find one for donation at your local thrift store? Remember jumping on the bed as a kid? A little controlled bouncing goes a long way. Make sure to hold their hands while they are doing it. Just do not let them jump without you there to supervise or you may end up with an unplanned visit to the emergency room.

Are you seeing a pattern in the therapies? A lot of the time, there is no cost. You are using yourself and the things you have around the home. The only cost is your time. If you do not feel you have the time, teach others in the family or your child's caregivers.

What if there is a particular piece of equipment you would really like to have, for instance, a mini trampoline? Ask around and see if anyone has an old one that they want to give away. You may be surprised at how many people will respond to a call for help regarding therapy for your son or daughter. Do not be afraid to ask. This is the beginning of you becoming a strong advocate for your child. Also, do not forget to check second-hand stores, like Goodwill. I was there this past weekend and saw two mini trampolines for sale at a fraction of what a new one would cost.

Take the time to play with your child. It's more important than you can possibly imagine, and I promise it will be worth it!

A Sensory Diet

Next, let's talk about the words "sensory diet." Claire Heffron in a 2019 article from Healthline.com explains that "A sensory diet is a program of sensory activities kids perform during the day to ensure they're getting the input their bodies need." These activities will help them calm and, hopefully, address what stimulations their bodies are craving.

To understand what a sensory diet is you need to understand Sensory Processing Disorder (SPD). A child can have SPD and not be autistic. However, if your child is on the autism spectrum, they will most likely have some form of SPD.

I explained SPD to our son in this way (when he was old enough to understand). The nerves that carry impulses to your brain are like highways with lots of cars. With SPD the highway can have a huge traffic jam limiting the car's ability to carry the message to the brain of what you should be feeling. SPD can work in the reverse too by having highways that are so big that too many cars carry too much information to the brain at once causing a person to feel overwhelmed. To make things even more difficult for the person experiencing SPD, their symptoms can fluctuate from day to day. One day they can be over-sensitive and the next day under-sensitive!

Our son really got hit hard with SPD. Here are some brief examples:

- Every bath night was a fight. If even the tiniest of lint from a sock or dust bunny got into the water he would refuse to get in. The water temperature had to be "just right." It would take quite a lot of convincing to get him into the tub. Then getting him out of the tub was another hurdle because he didn't want to get out. The room was too cold and it hurt his skin to dry off with a towel.

- When he needed a haircut - he couldn't stand the feeling or the sound of the scissors or clippers cutting his hair. These overstimulations made it difficult to have his hair cut in a barbershop. I would cut his hair at home, one small part at a time over a period of about a week while he was distracted with a toy in the tub. No hair could fall in though! One quick snip and done for that day.

- Food - nothing crunchy would be accepted. Nothing gooey, gelatinous, or wet would be accepted. There is a whole chapter in this book devoted to his food sensitivity problems and how we helped him conquer many of them over time.

- Crowds and loud noisy places were also a problem: these caused too much hearing stimulation. It was the same with singing - no one was allowed to sing around him.

These were just a few of his issues. What does all this sensory overload lead to? Refusal, refusal, refusal! Refusal behavior becomes a constant and difficult companion. After all, how do we as adults respond to stimuli that are unpleasant? We avoid doing whatever we did that caused the discomfort!

This is where the sensory diet comes into play. Repetitive exposure to stimuli is what we shoot for to help kids become accustomed to what they are feeling. A sensory diet targets the reason a behavior is occurring and can help an individual become accustomed to and less reactive to the stimuli that are unpleasant to them.

Here is an example. To improve our son's aversion to touching things squishy or wet, we started with playdough. What kid doesn't want to play with this type of squishy fun? Ours. Getting him just to touch it, let alone roll and squish the dough took months of therapy. Next up, we tried rolling cars through paint or whipped cream. He adored cars and trains and would lie on the floor moving a vehicle back and forth watching the wheels turn for long periods of time. We took his love for cars and would hold his hand and drive the car through the paint. Oops, a little got on the car. Oops, a little got on his hand. This all sounds quite calm and civilized as I am typing it. I assure you that wailing, screaming, and running away were all part of the therapy as well. This type of therapy was usually anything but peaceful and could become a very messy business. It was also exhausting. We would first use a deep pressure therapy, then move to a more difficult one, and finish with another deep pressure. Calming, challenging, calming - this alternating sequence was key. The first time he didn't scream because a little paint got on his hand - awesome!

A good sensory diet should be a written plan for you to follow with your child. You will find that you are doing that calming, challenging, calming sequence throughout the day at the same time every day. We started with a schedule of working with our son after each meal and at bedtime. Taking only a few minutes of our time, several times a day, worked really well for us and for him, when we stuck to the plan.

Right now, a voice in your head may be saying - four times a day - no way. Many of you have full-time jobs and your time is limited. If so, create a shorter version that works around your schedule. Teach others to handle his sensory diet as well when you cannot be there. For us, the most convenient time to work with our son was in the morning and at bedtime. If a third session was worked in at lunch that was "icing on the cake."

A Rice Box

Part of our sensory diet, and another favorite of ours, was our rice box. We had one big enough for him to sit in, but smaller versions are just as good. A rice box is exactly what the name implies - a box filled with uncooked rice. Having a lid is kind of important as you really want it to be sealed when not in use. (Ants like rice boxes too!) Buried in the rice are things that a child might find interesting to play with. For our son, we had cars and dinosaurs. He would sit in the box with only a diaper on, and I would encourage him to root through and find a toy. A sheet under the box would keep rice grains from getting everywhere and make cleaning up easy.

We would play in the rice for a certain amount of time and then transition out with warnings. His warnings would begin fifteen minutes before cleaning up. They would continue at five-minute intervals until the last two minutes when he would again be warned that time to clean up was coming soon. These warnings were crucial in getting him out of the box without an argument. I didn't want to spoil the fun with a fight at the end because he didn't receive warnings to help transition. This was very calming for him and fun.

Sign Language and Speech Therapy

A big part of what we were learning from early intervention was how to provide a sensory diet. That was not the only hurdle they helped us to navigate. As I mentioned, our son didn't babble. He didn't talk at all. What we thought were temper tantrums from not getting his way were actually his way of expressing his frustration over not being able to communicate his needs. He knew what he wanted to tell us but couldn't make the words form. After a few months of early intervention, speech therapy was added as a third visit per week.

We were introduced to sign language and bought an introductory DVD series called "Signing Time" to help teach us all. He loved the videos hosted by Rachel Coleman from Two Little Hand Productions. She uses music to teach sign language.

I missed the very first time he used a sign to communicate what he wanted. We were at a friend's house on a playdate. My husband was in the basement playing with the other kids. (We couldn't leave our son alone with other children when he was very young. One of us was always with him.) There was a ball pit inside an inflatable pool in the basement. Our son would throw out the balls and my husband would scoop them up and drop them back in. Our son signed "more balls" to my husband when he stopped for a break. What a moment! My feelings went from absolute happiness because he was beginning to use sign language to envy because my husband got to see him sign first. Our son picked up the signs quickly after that and soon the temper tantrums from frustration regarding communication were just a memory. My husband and I used to joke that he would be signing "Yes please" on his wedding night! For anyone concerned about signing versus verbal expression, the signing fades out as the talking begins. The switch happens quite naturally.

The speech therapy continued: signing was only part of the therapy. According to AutismSpeaks.org, "Speech-language therapy addresses challenges with language and communication." A child can receive therapies that include a focus on facial expressions, body language, tone of voice, and much more. While most children pick up the clues on how to interact with each other very easily and early on, our son needed to be taught how to interact with others. What is considered acceptable and what is considered unacceptable did not come naturally to him. For instance, when seeking deep pressure while playing with others, he would often crash into them. He needed to understand that crashing into people is not acceptable behavior and can hurt others. As an example of a therapy to counter this behavior: "Blue Car" asks "Red Car" to play. Play starts with racing and following the leader. A crash occurs - the Red Car says, "That hurt" and "We can't play if you hurt me." Play resumes unless a hit occurs again. If a hit occurs again, the fun is taken away as the red car "leaves" because he "doesn't like crashes". The many and varied nuances that constitute speech therapy still amaze me to this day. Our son had speech therapy until he entered the seventh grade. We were very fortunate to have the same speech therapist all the way through elementary school.

Pretend Play And "The Box"

One of my favorite forms of therapy was a giant empty box made of heavy cardboard. Pretend play (role play) did not come naturally to our son. Pretending to be someone else (such as a fireman, an astronaut, or a race car driver) needed to be taught to him and shown that this could be fun. Using a large box that he could climb into on his own as an aid to imagine a different environment was a simple form of play and resulted in some fantastic therapy. Turn the box over and you have a cave. Rock the box back and forth and you are on a boat in the ocean. Attach a hose and it's a fire truck: we used an old short pool hose. Launch into space with your stuffed animals and go to another planet in your spaceship box. Of course, his favorite stuffed animals were along for all the adventures and how they reacted to him and their fellow animals was a key to some really good learning.

This large box stayed in our living room for several years. We didn't just use the box for pretend play: his fine motor skills really needed work, and we used the outside of the box for that as well. He learned how to hold a crayon to draw a window, stars, a ladder, or color a shape on the box. The simple act of pulling off a sticker from a sheet and placing the sticker on the box was another learned skill. If he was feeling too stressed, the box with a blanket and stuffed animal was a safe place to relax and decompress. The variety of uses of the box was limited only by the imagination of the adult who was orchestrating playtime.

This box was the center of a large part of his therapy. Its importance and the amount of time we spent working with the box, led me to write a short children's story called *A Home for Box*. This story is about a box that dreams of becoming a part of a family. (My goal was to create a children's book that could "teach" parents about basic therapy and encourage a child to never give up on their dreams.)

I loved that box and can tell you without any shame that there was some crying involved when we finally put it into the recycling bin!

Day Care/Preschool Before Age Three

As mentioned before, our son was unable to attend any kind of organized events with other children. No Gymboree, no story time at the library, no daycare or preschool organization for our son: there was no real focus, just refusal behavior. He couldn't talk and would hit with his hands or toys. I compensated by finding places where we would be together and he could enjoy himself and have some interaction that was monitored or orchestrated by me. Two of our favorite places were the local park and the library's children's book area. We also went to our local indoor mall to burn off energy. All of these environments permitted me to be right there with him monitoring all of his behavior and correcting or removing when necessary. When we met a new adult and child, I always spoke to them about our son having autism and how he was still learning about social interactions. Most parents were very sympathetic and didn't mind that we spent some time playing with their child while teaching our son how he should interact appropriately with play partners.

At first, there was no sitting and chatting with another parent while our child played with theirs. I was right there in the mix directing the play as our early intervention specialist had taught me. This wasn't always perfect, but this option was the best we had at the time. There was one unfortunate incident at the local park. Our son had been playing well with a little girl in the jungle gym until she stepped a little too close. I wasn't close enough to stop him when he hauled off and smacked her across the face. Boy was that little girl's father angry! He didn't care that our son had autism. I, through our son, had injured his little girl. Yikes! How to handle it? I apologized profusely to the man and the little girl on behalf of our son but didn't bother to explain more. Dad wasn't interested. Our son was told that he had lost his privilege of playing at the park today because he hit. We do not hit. Kicking and screaming, we left the park (with me holding him that special way so I wouldn't be hurt). I think I lectured him on it all the way home.

Remember how I stated earlier the WHY is important? Being armed with knowing why he hit made things easier for me when providing a consequence for his actions without being angry. The little girl inadvertently invaded his personal space, and his response was automatic. However, obviously, hitting is not an acceptable response in polite society and our job was to teach him this.

Consequences, while so important when you are raising a typical child, are even more important when raising an autistic one. It is imperative that you let your child know what your expectations are and what will happen if he or she does something wrong. You need to discuss this with them prior to anything happening.

For instance, before leaving the car to go to the playground in the park, I would state something like this: "Mommy is really happy that we get to go to the park today and play. But, if you hit anyone, we will have to leave the park, and we can't stay." As he got older, asking him, "What did mom just say?" helped with understanding. Making him repeat important instructions back to me let me know he actually heard and comprehended what was said to him.

Always tell your child the truth. "If you hit, we will have to go home." Period. No discussion, no arguing. Tell him or her that they are responsible for their own actions. Tell them that their action caused this consequence. *Never threaten to do something if you are not prepared for them to call you on it, because they will!* You have to be strong and always follow through with the consequences. You are the adult in this relationship and will need to "stubborn out" your child. Is this easy? No way! Does this ever stop? Eventually, if you are consistent, the frequency of challenges will slow down to only once in a while. While your children are young, though, be prepared for constant challenges. If you want to maintain your sanity, set your "hard" limits sensibly and pick your battles. Even now as a young adult, our son occasionally tries to blame someone else for his failings. I tell him the same thing every time: "No this is your fault. You chose to behave/act in this way. Now you must deal with the consequences of your actions."

Nothing irritates me more than when a parent says to little Johnny or Joanie, "Don't do that or I'll have to take you home," and they do not follow through. When the incident happens again, the parent either ignores it or says again, "Don't do that." How do you expect your child to respect what you say if you do not follow through with what you tell them you are going to do? In essence, you are lying to your child. Once they realize you are not serious about discipline or consequences, it's all over for you.

A word of caution is necessary here. If every little behavior is a problem and you are constantly making your child feel like he or she behaved wrong, you will raise a very insecure child who feels they can never do anything right. Let the little things that are not as important go for a while, until they either become the big things or until you have handled the bigger things and are now ready to work on other behaviors. Walking the fine line of discipline is difficult for parents, which leads to a search for alternatives to the old go-to-your-room punishment. One of those alternatives is ABA therapy.

ABA therapy (Applied Behavior Analysis Therapy) has many nuances. Some people rave about ABA therapy: others find it offensive and wrong. It will be up to you to decide. Autismspeaks.org has a good basic explanation of what ABA therapy entails. They state, "The goal is to increase behaviors that are helpful and decrease behaviors that are harmful or affect learning." This involves things such as positive reinforcement, communicating before a behavior happens, and the consequences of said behavior when it does occur. The aspect of this therapy we found most effective involved rewarding the good behavior that is exhibited and celebrating your child's successes with them. The idea is that by rewarding good behavior, the child will strive to exhibit the good behavior again to get rewarded until a habit is formed. My husband called it "bribery." I didn't care. This type of ABA therapy when done correctly, worked very well for our son in his early years.

Consistency Is The Key

We soon learned how important consistency was for our son's daily routine. A month after our son was born, I began a bedtime routine. Every night at the same time, we would go up to the bedroom. After we were in bed, we read a story or two to him. Promoting my love for reading, and passing it on to our son, was important to me. My research from long ago instilled in me the importance of maintaining a consistent bedtime routine in order to get your kids to go to bed with as little trouble as possible. We read every night. Eventually, we began to take turns reading and then he finally told me he wanted to read the book himself. Because of this routine, the "squishing" therapy was easy to add to our bedtime practice. 9:00 p.m., every night, we were in his room reading and winding down. I tried putting him to bed earlier, but he just wasn't ready. Even when we were on vacation, we kept to the same routine. A consistent bedtime routine becomes a true source of comfort for a child; and bedtime, although time-consuming for us, was a delightful and rewarding experience for many years.

A Preschool Opportunity

When our son was about two and a half years old an opening occurred in a grant program at a local preschool. We applied for our son to be considered for the opening through early intervention: otherwise, we never would have known the grant existed. It allowed a special needs student to attend daycare with a one-on-one aide to help. Our son was accepted into the program. For six months before he could start at the local public school at age three, he would be going to a preschool two days a week for a few hours. This gave me a much-needed break and set us up well for when our local public school asked to "evaluate" him for acceptance into the preschool age three program. One short visit from the head of the Child Study Team of the public school was all that was needed for her to say, yes, he can start as soon as he turns three years old.

For over a year, early intervention specialists were with our son two to three times a week providing much-needed speech and occupational therapy. They were my biggest advocates and taught me so well that I was able to continue the therapies on the days they did not visit and beyond in later years. When our son turned three, all of this ended. We were cast adrift into the public educational system. Can you say culture shock? For me, it felt like I'd lost my childhood "blankie."

Chapter 4

The First Year of Preschool

When my son turned three, we still didn't have an official diagnosis and that made for some angst on my part - would he be accepted into the local public school's preschool program? Only children age three who had a learning disability in two or more areas would be accepted. Knowing that our son really needed to be in the program, I was prepared to fight to get him accepted. However, it was apparent, after he was observed by the school's Child Study Team, that he qualified. He still wasn't speaking, couldn't interact with his peers, required a one-on-one person to keep him focused, and more.

We were finally able to have our son evaluated for autism at a local children's hospital. The evaluation process took almost a full day. At the end, we were told that he didn't have autism. The doctor said he would probably have a learning disability, but we would have to wait and see how things progressed. Years later when visiting another neurologist, we found out that his actual results were borderline; and, yes, he was and is autistic.

For my first official meeting with the Child Study Team, I brought a binder full of his evaluations, doctor reports, and records. My goal for the meeting was to show up looking like a woman who was not fooling around and who was highly organized. (Half the battle is appearing like you know your stuff.) The early intervention professional had prepped me on what to expect. Nervously arriving early on that day with my binder but outwardly with a relaxed, intelligent attitude, I joined them at the table. They never knew what thoughts were going through my head. (In reality, all I wanted to do was vomit before, during, and afterward!)

Integration into the preschool program was an adventure. My first request was to sit in on one of the classes for a little while as an observer. Walking into a room with nine very well-behaved little girls was disheartening. They sat in a circle around their teacher while she explained the weather, discussed the day of the week, and read a story. Not one of them moved a single inch from where they sat for the entire time. You could hear a pin drop in the class. The only voice was that of the teacher. I thought, "They are in for such a surprise" and was concerned that our son was not going to fit into this cute little class. Child Study arranged to have him further evaluated, and he was to receive both speech and occupational therapy one time a week. One time a week didn't seem like enough, but there was no cost. Hopeful that these new therapists would teach us additional ways to help our son, we gave our consent to begin. (After all, I thought, look how much we learned from early intervention.)

The day came to put him on the bus and head out. He was scheduled for the afternoon class. Again, not my choice: and my request for a morning class was denied. My mother insisted on being there with me for support. This seemed silly to me. I was quite all right with having two to three hours of my day, five days a week ALL TO MYSELF.

He got on the bus with little coaxing and they drove off. The moment they drove away with him, the tears started. Mine, not his. They took our baby! They know nothing about his needs. Apparently, I was not as "all right" as I thought. My mom gave me hugs and took me to lunch to change my focus to something else instead of dwelling on how he did on his first day. After that, there were no more tears; but every once in a while, seeing a mom with her three-year-old would make me get a little angry because mine wasn't with me all the time. Silly as that may seem, feelings are not always logical. Adapting to separation can be as difficult for the parent, initially, as for their child.

Lessons We All Had To Learn

The school's first lesson in learning about our son was about bussing. He was the first picked up and the last to be dropped off. This meant that he rode the bus for 45 minutes (during his usual nap time) before he got to school. Of course, he fell asleep and then could not transition upon being woken up early from what should have been his two-hour nap. They had to deal with all the screaming, crying, and violence associated with this little problem. This all could have been avoided - but no one would listen to me. The suggestion was made many times that an early morning class would be better for him. "No, they were not able to do that." Suggestions were also made several times that a shortened bus ride would solve their problem. Eventually, if the problem had not been rectified, we would have sent a letter requesting a meeting. Until the actual people who would be dealing with our child really got to know me, they considered me an "uneducated" parent about our child's disability. Sorry if I step on some toes here - but this has been my experience and continues to be my experience when beginning a relationship with someone who does not know me or our son. Are there parents out there who really do not know anything about their child's disability? Sure, there are a few. However, they are a small percentage. After all, if you choose to be an advocate for your child and want him or her to be successful, you reach out for information or ask for help. It's been mentioned by many educators and medical professionals that I'm not a typical parent. What does that mean? Learning as much as possible about our son's disability is a very hands-on approach for me. I do not consider myself unique.

After three weeks, the bus driver told me that they were going to change things around a bit and have his ride shortened to about ten minutes. He would be the last to be picked up before heading out to the school. *What a great idea!*

Right before Christmas break, we received a call from the school principal. Our son had pulled the fire alarm during their holiday party. Fortunately, my husband was home to handle the call. (Sometimes it's better to let a more reserved person handle things.) He was pissed but polite because the principal went on and on about how this couldn't happen again, the cost involved, etc. It surprised us that:

1. There was no cover on the pull alarm in the preschool class;

2. Our son had stacked several things on top of each other and had proceeded to climb them to reach the uncovered alarm; and

3. No one was watching him while he did this!

Yes, it was much better that my husband spoke to the principal.

Also at this time, our son would come home smelling like a very nice perfume. The floral scent was the perfume his preschool teacher wore. At first, the smell upset me. Some other woman was holding our son! It took a little time for me to understand that this was a very special woman. She was taking the time to hold and comfort our son during his difficult and stressful moments. My irritation disappeared once I acknowledged my jealousy and replaced it with a sense of gratitude. She also volunteered to take our son to the bathroom to help potty train him. I later found out, after he was moved from her classroom that this was not something that she was supposed to do. His new teacher told us that the school nurse would have to take care of it. The nurse's office was on the other side of the school and this resulted in significant disruption to his training. Often, he would come home with poop in his pants or smelling like urine. Triple Paste became the go-to ointment for his poor little abused bum. Extra diapers along with a change of clothes, just in case, were always sent to school with him. His diapers often leaked. Sometimes, he even came home wearing a shirt or pants that were not his own. They were pulled from the nurse's stockpile of donated clothes. I paid it forward in later years by donating items myself for those who were in the same position we had been in years before.

Our son actually wasn't fully potty trained (both #1 and #2) until he was about five years old. This made my husband crazy! Me, not so much. It's not uncommon for even neurotypical children in preschool to not be fully potty trained. I knew that he would eventually learn to use the bathroom. Was it frustrating? Sure! Was his lack of training embarrassing at times? Yes, absolutely. Remembering the lyrics to a song from the Signing Time DVDs helped me keep things in perspective. Rachel Coleman sings beautifully about how her child will learn what she needs to learn in her own time. That time may take longer than you would like or what people will expect, but your child will eventually learn what they need to do. This life lesson still runs through my head even now that he is twenty years old. Eventually, our son did learn to use the bathroom and stopped having "accidents" in his pants. He learned in his own time and now it is just a distant memory for us. Be patient and keep trying. Your child will be successful eventually.

A New Teacher And The Train Chart

About halfway through the first school year, the Child Study Team moved our son into a different preschool classroom. Why they did this was never explained, which was frustrating. Either his teacher retired or they wanted our son to be in a classroom where there was an aide to help the teacher. We were just told, "This class is a better fit for him" when asked.

His new teacher was not as warm and fuzzy as his first. Her aide was also our son's bus aide. Both had strong personalities and were good at keeping a class together and moving along. On the positive side, his teacher was good with communication. She started communicating with me through the school agenda. The school provided agendas for free to all students. The agenda was wonderful and awful at the same time. The communication aspect was great; unfortunately, the notes were mostly about his struggles.

Green, yellow, red - those were the colors for behavior. Our son only rarely had a green day, and almost never two green days in a row. I am a great believer in following through regarding behavior. If you didn't finish a project in school, you have to finish the project at home. If you hit another child at school, there were repercussions regarding that behavior when you got home. Still, I didn't want our son to feel like he was getting in trouble every day: that can be demoralizing for any child. That the teacher took her own time to communicate with me every day was great, but it was very hard to read about all the difficulties he was having.

In an effort to focus on the positive, I created a reward train with each day being one train car. Drawing pictures of train cars and laminating them was the first step. Next came a page with a train track, which was also laminated. Finally, velcro was attached to each train car and the other piece to the tracks, resulting in a reusable reward chart.

The chart was placed in a prominent position in our kitchen. At first, if he had a green or yellow day at school, he could put a train car up on the chart. When he reached five cars, he could choose a prize from his prize box.

Creating a prize box for young children is easy. He loved cars, dinosaurs, bugs, and trains. These could be obtained cheaply at the dollar store and made him so happy. I couldn't use food items because his diet was so limited. (Of course, if you are not dealing with food issues, that could be an option for rewards.) No comment from me on whether the snacks should be healthy or not: it's once a week. Use what works best for your child to motivate him or her.

As time went on, we progressed to requiring him to have a green day to place a train on the chart. After that, we moved up to ten train cars. At this point, his "green" days did not have to be in a row. That was another step toward promoting positive behavior at a later date. I didn't know at the time, but this was really similar to an aspect of ABA therapy.

Even using this method to motivate, the year was a frustrating one with regard to behavior. In addition, we had a small problem with the aide. As was previously mentioned, our son's aide was also his bus aide. His bus driver was a very nice woman who liked to talk. She began to tell me how our son's day went every day. Each day she began to get increasingly specific. At first, I didn't think anything of it. However, after a particularly long conversation with the driver one day, her comments began to make me angry. How did this woman know so much about our son and what business was it of hers what kind of day he had? If she knew, who else knew? Apparently, the aide was having conversations about our son on the bus (in front of other children and our son) about all the things he did wrong during the day. I made a call to the Director of The Child Study Team where, politely, I asked her to have a conversation with the aide about this inappropriate behavior. The bus driver stopped talking to me every day about our son's behavior, and I didn't miss those conversations one bit.

Other Influences

Eventually, meetings with his speech and occupational therapists were scheduled. Both therapists were excellent and were very willing to pass on things that could be worked on at home regarding the difficulties he was having at school. In fact, they were shocked but delighted that I expressed such an interest. Another lesson we learned-it's not only your child's teacher that can provide you with ideas to help your child with their difficulties. We were really lucky that we had the same speech therapist and occupational therapist for most of our son's elementary school education. They stayed with him all the way until he transitioned into middle school. The elementary school psychologist also became an important person in our lives and another "go-to" person who could help when we needed it.

His occupational therapist helped with his middle school transition and made sure she was available to us if we needed anything. It's always awkward for me when meeting a new person who will be working with our son. People can't help but make assumptions, and assumptions about me or our son have often been proven wrong. Sometimes, I just want to walk up and say, "Hi. You don't know me, but I have a lot of knowledge about autism and I'm really involved in anything that has to do with my child. You are going to get to know me very well."

As the year went on, our son began to imitate the behaviors of other students. This was good and bad. This was good if he mimicked a student who was behaving well but bad if he mimicked a student who was behaving poorly. His ability to mimic behavior and make the behavior his own is a true gift. To this day, he observes how others are acting around him and mimics their behavior to better "fit in." This is one of the things that makes it hard for everyone to actually realize that he is autistic. He is very reserved. Many people think he is shy or uninterested. In reality, he is observing the world around him and evaluating how he should act in a given situation. Fortunately, we were able to instill in him a solid sense of right and wrong, and we did not have to worry about him mimicking the wrong behavior very often.

The mimicking wasn't just of his fellow students: it was adult behavior as well. For instance, he came home one day and started banging his hand on a nearby table saying loudly "Attention! Attention!" This continued over a period of weeks. I finally asked him what he was doing and his response was, "I'm doing what Teacher...(name)...does." His aide would get attention in the classroom by doing the same thing. This must have appealed to him. Thankfully, when the school year was over that behavior faded away.

This was the year his speech development accelerated. He continued to use sign language but also spoke the words to communicate. What a relief this was to both my husband and me. We thought he would never talk! We would have found ways to work around the fact that he couldn't verbally communicate if that had continued to be an issue. Thankfully, his verbal difficulties had resolved.

Unfortunately, however, a new problem was brought to our attention. Our son could not attend school assemblies. His hearing was so sensitive, the room so loud and overwhelming, that they couldn't even get him in the door. (This is common with autistic children) Some noise-canceling headphones were obtained; and after working with him for most of the year, his teachers finally were able to get him to enter the room and sit on someone's lap for a short time near the door.

He didn't have a one-on-one aide. The school didn't really want to supply this, and we didn't feel a one-on-one aide was necessary. There was a single aide in the classroom for all the children. Since the class size was relatively small, sharing an aide was fine. I wanted him challenged and integrated into a classroom with typical children his age. This was my personal choice. For your child, depending on the extent of their disability and the circumstances in the classroom, your choice may be different. However, I do feel strongly that integration into a classroom with typical children is key to development in the early years. There is considerable data that suggests this is very important. Alana.org provides a paper and study written by Dr. Thomas Hehir and others entitled, *A Summary of the Evidence on Inclusive Education.*

It is an extensive read, but some key points discussed were language development, academic performance, and social and emotional development. All these were shown to benefit from integration.

Inclusion isn't right for every child. You should do what feels right for you and your child, but do your homework and bring that homework with you if you have to meet with your Child Study Team. The excuse that there is just no money in the district for a one-on-one aide is not acceptable. If your child requires such a person to be able to function in the least restrictive environment, then keep pushing them to supply one. Learn about your child's rights in your state and be prepared to defend them. An Internet search for your child's right in public education will provide you with many sources to access. If you don't feel comfortable speaking knowledgeably about your child's rights, search for an advocate to help you.

Our son finished his first year of preschool and had little art projects to prove this taped to the walls in our house. There were only a few. I'm sure his aide or teacher did most of the work, but we were very proud when he "finished" any project and brought his artwork or "writing" home. Over the years, we had tape marks on the paint all over the kitchen and living room walls. It was worth every mark on those walls to show him how proud we were of his work.

Sharing Colds And Viruses

One final comment about entering the first year in the public school system - WELCOME TO THE WORLD OF GERMS! Yep, be prepared. This is very typical for any child entering any type of classroom for the first time. The first year was hell for us. Any virus that came along, our child would get. If your child has older siblings, they probably will be exposed earlier and the year might not be as bad. To be prepared, here are a few suggestions.

Have the usual medications on hand before the school year starts so you only have to reach for your liquid Tylenol or Motrin when that fever strikes at 2:00 a.m. This is a simple practice that will keep the frustration level down. It's hard enough seeing your child sick, but having to get to the store to get the over-the-counter medication that can help them just makes the whole situation more difficult than it has to be if you are prepared ahead of time.

Try and take care of yourself as much as possible too. Yes, raising a child with special needs is exhausting, and there is that temptation to put our needs at the very end of the importance list. Every once in a while, you need to put your needs at the top! Not just physically, but mentally! Remember, if you go down, you can't take care of anyone else! Take that extra vitamin C and your regular multivitamin religiously. Do not skip your routine doctor visits. Try to get as much sleep as you can, and ask for help from family members to give you a break every once in a while. I know that this can be really difficult. Our son woke me twice a night every night for almost ten years. There was a pillow and blanket on the floor of his room for me to catch some sleep when the bed became too small for the two of us. I took naps when possible and went to bed when he did to ensure I had enough sleep. Taking care of yourself just may help you fight off some of those viruses and be better prepared when your child succumbs to the next one that comes along. Just like you do for your child, keep over-the-counter cold medication stocked in your cabinet for yourself. Make this a habit and replenish medications every September.

The first time our son got a stomach virus, we ended up in the hospital where he was on an IV to rehydrate him. On the way to the hospital, he vomited in my husband's car. He vomited over my shoulder as he was pulled out of the car. He vomited in the emergency room. (Well, you get the idea.) Sickness is hard for a parent of a typical child. Add in special needs and sickness can be frightening for both parent and child. Take care of yourself so that when you are needed, you will be there for your child. Our son has christened every new car that my husband has owned with vomit. My husband is totally appalled each time. I try not to laugh.

Summer Disruption

Summer came, and we were not offered inclusion in a summer school program since he was only in preschool. There wasn't anything in the area that our son could attend. In our case, any suggestions made by the Child Study Team were not realistic. They couldn't help. Despite a year of preschool, he couldn't attend a class of any kind without a great deal of supervision and really didn't have an interest in doing so. My church didn't offer anything. I fell back on the local park and our library. Briefly, we tried to supplement his learning, but he was very resistant. When September came, there was relief and apprehension regarding starting the next year of preschool. Before we could start, however, we had to deal with his pesky eating problem.

Chapter 5

The Eating Program Adventure

O ur son had some significant issues with food. He was a picky eater. Actually, calling him a picky eater doesn't even come close to describing his difficulties in the early years. Before his second year of preschool started, we had some really troubling doctor visits regarding his eating habits. Our son's heightened sensitivity to taste, texture, visual stimulation, and touch had limited him to only two food choices. He was existing on a diet of french toast (brand-specific) and bananas. He only drank water and very rarely some milk. We were urged to seek help from the local children's hospital by our pediatrician. They had an ABA-based feeding program that was highly recommended.

Being told there was a program for children with eating problems was a great relief to us. I could not get him to eat anything but french toast and bananas, which left me feeling totally inadequate as a parent. It was so frustrating! Our son refused to let me feed him, refused to use utensils, and would absolutely not eat anything else. He had to eat, and I did not think much about the old saying, "He'll eat when he's hungry." He would just *not eat*. This was not an option for us, and we later learned that this was the right decision. Our son, like many children with autism, did not feel hunger - or more accurately did not recognize what hunger felt like and then equate the feeling to eating food for relief at his age. A medical professional at the hospital said that these children can actually starve themselves rather than eat foods they do not like. Scary!

The closest children's hospital was in a nearby city. I began the process of getting him evaluated for the program but was quite apprehensive. Not for the reason you might think: the program itself didn't really worry me because any anxiety was alleviated after speaking with a parent whose child successfully completed the program. The parent had nothing but good things to say!

My problem was that driving in this large city gave me very bad anxiety. My anxiety was so terrible that my husband drove us every time we had an appointment in the city. I would have a small panic attack every time, even just thinking about driving into any high-traffic area: in the morning what should have been a twenty-minute drive, took an hour to an hour and a half. Even though this was so important for our son's health, coming to terms with the stress associated with the drive was difficult for me. This was before the purchase of a cell phone or a GPS.

Fortunately, we qualified to stay in the city at a local Ronald McDonald House. A friend who knew the city well offered to take me there to check the House environment. They were graciously welcoming and gave us a full tour. What an incredible place. Our cost would be $40 for the week and dinner was provided every night free of charge. We would have our own room, most of the time with our own bathroom, as well. The House had rows of large refrigerators and freezers where we could store our own food and a giant play area for the kids. It was very impressive!

Our son was easily accepted into the eating program and our insurance would pay a large portion of the cost. At the time, the cost to attend the program was approximately $10,000. Our portion to pay was about $2,000. The pieces were falling in place for us to attend. We would start at the beginning of August and he would only miss about a week of school in September.

Before speaking about our great adventure, let me tell you about the results and why it was worth the cost and effort. We graduated from the program after five weeks with our son eating twenty-two different foods! They sent us home with a plan to continue the program, and we received extensive training. Not only did I witness my own child's success, but saw several families finding similar success with their children. This was by far, one of the best things we ever did for our son. But, it wasn't easy.

The First Day

Each week would begin by driving into the city late Sunday afternoon. The traffic wasn't too bad at that time. They had a parking garage on the premises, so there was no worry about finding parking. We had a room with its own bathroom and our son received a small toy, a little black dog, as a gift when we arrived. He loved it. There was a large playroom with all kinds of toys to play with and a huge variety of movies to choose from that we could watch in our room. I felt confident that night when we went to bed that everything would be okay.

The next morning, I drove to the hospital from the House. Unfortunately, "move-in day" at the local college was the same day. Driving to and from the hospital that day still remains one of my worst experiences. Narrowly missing a bicyclist on the way back to the House nearly gave me a heart attack. I reached out to my caseworker at the House that evening, and we spoke about other options for transport to the hospital: She was kind and offered me alternatives. Fortunately, there was a commuter bus a short walk from the House that we could use at no cost. This bus was now my lifeline.

The first day of the program itself was by far the hardest. Parents were placed in a room with a one-way mirror so they could watch the activities with their child and an assigned care provider. You could hear and see everything in the sessions, which were recorded. They were very clear ahead of time about what to expect, but the reality of viewing the therapy for the first time was incredibly difficult. Some parents couldn't handle what they saw and backed out immediately after just one session.

The program worked like this: three meal sessions were scheduled each day. Our child had a container full of toys only he would get to play with during meal time. There was no mixing of toys with other children throughout the admission. A few of his favorite toys from home and a book with pictures of things we had done earlier in the summer were added to his box along with some new toys.

Very small pieces of one new food would be introduced at a time. The child was told the following. "If you take your bite, you get to play. If you don't take a bite, you don't get to play. If you still don't take a bite, I have to help you take a bite." If the child tried to hit the fork out of the provider's hand, another person would be called in to "block". This person stood behind the child and placed their arms in front of the child's shoulders so that their hands or arms would hit the blocker instead of the fork of food. The child was <u>not</u> held down. They were, however, in a chair with a tray, in such a way that they could not get out of the chair during the meal.

Some of you may be thinking right now, "How barbaric!" It's not, really. First, the child is usually crying and their mouth is already open. It was just a matter of dropping a very small piece of food into their mouth. If they spit the food out, no big deal: another piece would be given. If they threw up, the staff cleaned up and no fuss was made about it. The whole process was calmness and strength of will in the face of chaos. After one day of this therapy, our son understood what was expected of him. This surprised me, but I was very thankful that he seemed to get the hang of what was desired quickly. They never had to use blocking with him again and there were no more tears after the first day.

To start, breakfast was some scrambled eggs along with his favorite french toast or banana. He could choose which toy he wanted to play with each time he took a successful bite. I honestly can't remember what food was introduced at lunch or dinner that day. Our last meal was at 3:00 p.m., and we were back at the Ronald McDonald House by 4:00 p.m. Dinner was provided for me at the House, buffet style; and our son was allowed to have his favorite meal so he could sit with me during the evening dinner. Storing his favorite food was easy as they had both refrigerators and freezers for parents. The lunchroom was crowded, but our son didn't seem to care. He was too happy to be given his favorite food to react to anything else.

I cried myself to sleep that first night, exhausted and feeling utterly alone. My husband couldn't afford to take off five weeks to do this with us. The thought of being on my own for the next five weeks was overwhelming. My only company was a child who really didn't talk much to communicate. Knowing the importance of doing this for our son, I prayed that things would get better.

The Next Five Weeks

The second day turned out to be much better. Our son understood very quickly what he needed to do to play. The sessions were not always smooth sailing with all the foods introduced, but nothing was as difficult as that first day. We easily fell into a routine. First breakfast, then we would walk to a certain portion of the hospital to wait around for the next meal time. The hospital waiting room had a floor-to-ceiling marble machine. The device had bells and whistles and fascinated him. In addition, I carried a small bag of little toy trains, cars, and dinosaurs. Each week, a few new toys were introduced into the bag to keep things fresh. We would sit down to play and another child desperate for something to do would come by and ask to play too. Socialization accomplished!

The hospital also had a library with a few computers that the kids could use for some online learning games. I was permitted to take out some books that we could use each week as part of our bedtime routine. Between the computer and the time it took to pick out new books each week, he enjoyed the library. The transition was tricky getting him back to his room for the final meal, but he soon understood what was expected of him. Using what we learned through Early Intervention, he was given several warnings before we actually had to go. Promises that he could come back also helped.

Then, the week was over. Unfortunately, because we were not staying overnight at the hospital and had no meal challenges on Saturday and Sunday, we could not stay at the House over the weekend. They graciously let us stay over on Friday night, so we didn't have to fight the horrific traffic going home. Early Saturday morning I would pack everything all up and make the drive home. At home, I focused on chores, such as our laundry, cleaning the house a bit, updating my husband on our progress, and packing a bag for the following week. This was all done not knowing if the House would have a room available for us during the upcoming week. I had to call the House on Sunday in the late morning/early afternoon to see if a room would be available for us. Sometimes they would tell me to call back in an hour or two; nerve-wracking! Once given the okay, we made the trek back into the city on Sunday night. Each week there was anxiety over whether a room would be available, but it never became an issue. A room with my own bathroom for all but one of the five weeks was always available. One week, we had to share a communal bath and shower that was two steps from our room. In a situation like that, you make things work because you are so grateful to be staying there.

The staff truly cared about us and encouraged us to come to them to talk about anything. Several nights a week, college students would volunteer to come in and play with your child in the playroom. You didn't have to stay if you needed that time for some alone time to recharge. Free babysitting! I stayed anyway, but it was a relief not to be the person occupying our son's attention. The supply of DVDs to take to our room to watch at night was wonderful. Our routine was to play for a while after dinner and then head back to our room for a movie and then to bed. Even during these unusual circumstances, we kept to a consistent routine. Bedtime was, and continued to be, the same time every night. Routine and knowing what to expect are very important to an autistic person. Keeping to a routine helped a great deal with our son's transition difficulties during this experience. A routine also ensured that he received enough sleep to start refreshed the next day.

Hospital Outpatient Services

During our time at the hospital, we received other types of services in between meals as well. He received occupational therapy two times a week. Additional therapies that could be practiced at home were provided to us. A new sensory diet was supplied since we had not been using one for some time.

We also were referred to the Gastrointestinal Medicine department. Our son was having constipation problems and had some blood in his stool due to pushing so hard to get something out. He wasn't potty trained and still wore a diaper all the time. He was prescribed Miralax on a daily basis. The powder was mixed with his milk, which he began to drink at every meal. He didn't seem to mind it. He was on Miralax for years. A few years back, the news reported that this was dangerous for children and had side effects into adulthood. So far he hasn't had any long-term side effects from it. Healthline.com provides a brief explanation of Miralax and also states, "Although you don't need a prescription for Miralax, it's still a medicine." We consulted with our pediatrician and gastrointestinal physician regarding the dosage when we used the powder.

Our son has only positive memories from the whole five-week experience. He remembers the House and the hospital visits as a great adventure, although to be honest, he doesn't remember much detail. As mentioned earlier, we finished with twenty-two new foods in his diet after five weeks. That list included for the first time, chicken "McNuggets" and french fries from McDonald's.

Some of you may think, "Yuck! Why in the world would you want to introduce those foods?" Our son was almost four years old and had never been able to eat at a restaurant with us. We had to bring food with us everywhere we went, and this wasn't always easy to transport. I was positively giddy when we went to McDonald's for the first time on a mother-and-son date. This also made traveling with him so much easier and was the stepping-stone to getting him to try chicken at other restaurants as he grew older. We do not eat there anymore, because we do not need to. I do prefer healthier alternatives when eating out. However, at the time, learning to eat two foods from McDonald's was HUGE for us.

Preparing To Be On Our Own

Toward the end of the program, instructions were given on how to feed our son using the therapy that was being practiced. Before we left the program, I had to be comfortable with feeding him myself the right way. This wouldn't be forever. The sessions would fade out over time; but for the first month back at home, eating had to be very regimented.

I was nervous about feeding him the first time on my own at the hospital. This time, they were on the other side of the mirror; and it was my turn to practice the therapy. They were there if help was needed, but thinking about doing the feeding was formidable.

However, after watching the process for so many weeks, feeding our son just came naturally. He didn't object to me being the person who was feeding him and we both became comfortable with the whole process.

My husband was required to come and stay for two days to learn how things were done as well. The last week we were there, he stayed one night and the required two days. He was pretty amazed at how far we had come and how the program worked. He wasn't fully comfortable about having to feed our son this particular way, but he did what was required. In addition, he made me think more about what plans we should have in place for when we got home to continue the behavior therapy around eating.

My day-to-day survival mode had not allowed me to think that far ahead. My husband made me start asking questions because he asked questions. Our biggest concern was having some kind of chair that our son could not get out of when eating. We got lucky and found a used Rifton chair at a yard sale. Another alternative on the internet is a KeeKaroo High Chair. It's adjustable and can grow with your child. The chair holds up to 250 pounds and is about half the price of a Rifton chair.

The chair we found had seen some use but was still very serviceable. Wooden and quite cute, we used the chair until we didn't have to anymore. Then we donated the seat to someone else in need, paying it forward.

Things went reasonably well at home as we tried to keep the program going. I can't say I was able to introduce any more new foods using this method, but we did keep a food log and provided the log to the program staff at our next visit with the confidence of having done a decent job. This was, however, exhausting! When we were told it was time to gradually wean our son off of the program, the whole family couldn't have been happier. We were all ready for life to go back to normal - well, normal for us!

Chapter 6

The Second and Third Years of Preschool

We started his second year of preschool a bit late because of the feeding therapy. He had a new teacher and a new aide again. The second teacher and her aide from the prior year also retired. His new teacher was soft-spoken, yet strong. Our son would end up having this teacher for three years, although we didn't know this at the time.

As I hoped for a better year with his behavior, I asked her if she would consider using a communication logbook instead of the agenda. She seemed a bit surprised but readily agreed to this way of communicating. To my delight, she wrote often in the book. If there was something she wanted me to know about behavior, she would ask for suggestions or would let me know of a problem so follow-up at home could occur. Best of all, she didn't just focus on the negative. Instead, she focused more on celebrating his successes. Sure, he had quite a few more days in yellow or red than green, but this year was far different than the prior year.

Many years later, those log books provided me with insight for this book. Reviewing them, I was surprised by what I felt. Those books remind me that having the courage to ask for something often leads to more opportunities for our son's success.

That teacher wrote something in the book every day. This amazes me now: at the time, it was just taken for granted. What a commitment this teacher made to our child! The note may have only been a few sentences, but she wrote every single day. If she missed a day, which was infrequent, she apologized!

There was an entry from me every day as well and my notes were not just a short few sentences. What was I thinking? Since he had afternoon preschool, many of the entries were giving her an idea of how his morning behavior went at home. He was sick a lot that year, again. Several entries were about what kinds of things happened in the morning that might affect his behavior. Most of the time, they didn't but she would always write a thank you to me for keeping her informed. When she read my lengthy entries, she probably thought, "This poor woman really needs someone to talk to!"

Hitting and Refusal Behavior

The recurring theme, when things did go wrong, was that our son couldn't keep his hands to himself. Frustration was constant at the time, but the reason for the frustration was buried somewhere in my subconscious. How could I have totally forgotten all about his issues with hitting? He didn't just use his hands. If he had a toy in his hand, he would use that as well! Every time he came home with a report of an incident, the guilt would overwhelm me. Somehow, even though illogical, guilt consumed me over not having been able to prevent this event from happening. Sadness and fear were also constant companions and, of course, worry that things would never get better.

Behavior does get better. Impulse control has to be learned! It is not your fault he hit another child. As a responsible parent, thinking this way is normal. Please give yourself some space and perspective.

However, do not give your child a break. Each and every time this happens, you need to talk about hitting and what occurred. See if you can get them to tell you why they hit another person. "He took my toy!" or "He pushed me!" may be their response. Then, talk about a better way to have handled the situation. You can use cars or dolls to act out the occurrence and have your child show you what happened. You can also use these tools to demonstrate a better way to behave. I'm talking about using Social Stories through play. We often did this because it worked well for us.

If you haven't heard of social stories therapy, you need to explore this therapy by doing an Internet search. I found a good place to start was on the website RaisingChildren.net.AU. There is an article under Parent Guide: Therapies called, Social Stories. Some people have real success with social stories. Not every child can understand that a story is showing them how they should behave in a given social situation, but this therapy certainly is something to look into and try. Never turn away a particular therapy because you think or "know" it won't work. You never know what may reach your child.

Personally, we found that Social Stories worked best if we used them in play - not so much reading them to him as a story. Once, he voiced his frustration with us going over a story, by telling us he knew what he did wrong; and, "we didn't have to read that stupid story again."

With hitting, you also want to make sure you follow through with whatever consequences you have established before the incident. There should be no question in your child's mind that the consequences are a result of hitting another person. If you make things up as you go and do not have consistency, this will not be effective.

Eventually, they learn that hitting is not acceptable. The lesson can take time though. Try to be patient.

We also had issues with refusal behavior. Refusal to participate in activities such as circle time and refusal to eat and clean up after snack were noted often in the communication logbook. Class was only a two-and-half-hour period of time, but she would always try and give our son the chance to win back his green star. Sometimes he was able to do so. Even if he wasn't able to earn back his green star, she always ended her entry with the words, "I hope he has a better day tomorrow." Every day was a fresh new start with her, and she made sure that we all knew it.

Are you wondering how often we got a "bad" report from the teacher? In a good week, we usually had one difficult day that involved either refusal behavior, hitting, or both. In a week of more challenges on average, three out of five days there was some sort of incident. If this sounds familiar to you, then you know now that you are not the only one who has experienced this frustration. Been there, done that; it will be ok.

There are so many more good days than bad: I didn't see that at the time. Reading those same log books years later, the positive days really stood out. In retrospect, he had LOTS of great days and successes. Celebrate each day that's a success and make a big deal out of it! That way you and your child enjoy the "wins" and don't feel like you are constantly failing.

This period was when our reward train became an important tool. The train visually demonstrated the consequences of refusal behavior. Being unable to place a car was also the consequence of hitting, although there was always a conversation about that behavior and perhaps a small time limit on an activity that he enjoyed doing every night. I never went all or nothing with consequences and would not take his favorite activity away completely: for our son, that would have made things worse. We found that a better method was reducing his activity time. In our son's case, activity time was playing video games or watching television. At the end of activity time, he was reminded that his time was being cut short because he hit someone while he was in school. A 'green' day was a time for celebration when he placed a train car on the chart for that day. On a 'yellow' or 'red' day, we would discuss why we were sad that we couldn't put a train car up, and that tomorrow was another chance to do better.

Volunteering

Our son's preschool class was small. Parties were a great time to volunteer. I liked getting to know our son's peers and observing how the classroom worked. This made things easier when talking to him about cleaning up after snack - knowing exactly what was said and where things were placed. Emulating the words and the actions at home as a reinforcement helped him. Plus, those kids were all so stinking cute!

His final year in preschool, I volunteered to be head room mom. The teacher welcomed me into the classroom and worked with me to make school a more positive experience for not only our son but all students in her classroom. After all, the teacher spends a huge amount of time with your child. Having a teacher that is open to your suggestions and welcomes visits to their classroom is a gift!

Our son's three years of preschool involved a huge learning curve for all of us. There were difficulties, but now we had several partners in the school system who communicated with us to help our child become the best version of himself. To our surprise, our son made friends, some of which are still his friends today. He learned to attend assemblies and did not mind going to school. His final year of preschool was a good period of transition.

Solid relationships with his speech and occupational therapists developed into friendships: both were excellent and made me feel welcome. They didn't mind if periodically I reached out to them for guidance. If a particular behavior occurred in the classroom, we all worked together to try and figure out the "why" behind that behavior and how we could adjust it. Because our son's birthday fell in late fall, we were fortunate not to have made the early-age cut-off for kindergarten. As a result, our son is one of the oldest in his class. He turned eighteen early in his senior year. That third year of preschool allowed him to catch up with his peers emotionally, and he was so much more prepared for kindergarten because of it.

Summer

The summer between his second and third year of preschool, we sent him to a short private summer program that was several days a week. He had two years of preschool experience by then, and I felt that he would be okay with me dropping him off for a few hours. Of course, making sure they knew about his issues ahead of time was critical. The owners were very good with kids of all types and learning levels. The class was more of a 'play and craft' environment, which was disappointing because he would not be practicing the academic skills he learned from his second year in preschool. However, his time away gave me a needed break and gave our son socialization for part of the summer.

It was also during his last year of preschool that we discovered the "Sensory Playhouse." The Playhouse was fifteen minutes from our house and new to the area. Two women with special needs children of their own decided to create a fun and safe environment full of stations specially designed for children who were experiencing sensory issues. The Playhouse was an awesome place to visit. In the very back was a ball pit room. The floors were full of pillows to sit on and it was an open and comfortable space. Parents could spend time sitting on the floor near stations where their children played. For us, this new business became a haven to visit - a no-judgment zone where our son could play with other children. I could speak with parents who had children with special needs and also with parents who had typical children. Leaving our son still wasn't an option, but this wonderful space gave both of us an alternative to the park and the library. For the first time, summer break became something to look forward to. There were classes that our son could attend at the Playhouse. Parents were required to be present, but the class was behind a curtain: if they had any major issues, they could come and get me. Because of our son's sensory issues and his struggle with fine motor skills, crafts, and coloring were not his favorite thing to do and usually led to refusal behavior. We made a deal. If he did what he was asked to do in class, we could stay to play for a while. This worked some of the time. Other times, I took him home accompanied by the usual crying and screaming.

A New Neurologist

One afternoon, one of the owners took me aside to ask me gently about our son's diagnosis. I expressed my frustration over the lack of diagnosis and the "wait and see" attitude that was exhibited by the doctor at our local children's hospital. She recommended her children's neurologist at another hospital in a different state. The office was a further drive than to our local city but giving this a try seemed important. We were lucky, our health insurance at the time did not need a referral. I called the neurologist's office directly and received an appointment three months into the future. By now, we were used to the hurry up and wait that is often associated with getting an appointment for our child. We went on with life as best we could and looked forward to perhaps finding a doctor who could possibly answer the question, "Why is our son different?"

Chapter 7

Kindergarten

O ur school offered full-day kindergarten. Some of you do not have this amazing opportunity for your child. I am glad we did. For me, kindergarten was really an extension of preschool. He even had the same teacher! We were nervous - would he be able to control himself for a full day of school? Still, what a great way to prepare for first grade!

By now the school staff and I had a good working relationship, but not every teacher knew me. That year and every year thereafter into his senior year in high school, I would send a "hello" introduction email to his teacher(s) before school started. In those emails, there was a brief introduction and my contact information. Also included (in the early years) was a description of our son's difficulties and a reminder to the teacher that if there were any questions about his IEP to feel free to call me at any time. The email was always light and friendly. This conveyed that I was there to help, was open to ideas, and believed that we would have a great year. From experience, it doesn't hurt to start on a positive note.

Shortly after I sent my "hello" email for kindergarten, our son's kindergarten teacher gave her resignation notice and his preschool teacher was moved up to teach kindergarten. Hearing later through the school grapevine that the teacher who resigned didn't want to teach a class with any special needs students and that my email was the straw that broke the camel's back surprised me. To this day, I have no idea if that was true. If so, thank goodness she left. There are few things worse than having to work with an individual who isn't tolerant of your child's special needs. It's doable but isn't fun.

We were excited about the change. This meant that our son would not have to adjust to a new personality on top of adjusting to the rigors of a full-day kindergarten class. Ideally, I wouldn't want him to have the same teacher for more than two years in a row; however, for his situation at that time, the benefit seemed to outweigh the detriment.

What do I mean by "detriment?" When teachers change every year or two, your child gains the chance to learn how to adapt to a new personality "in charge." In adult life, we often have bosses or supervisors change on a regular basis. The ability to adapt to the change and work with a new person who has his or her own expectations regarding your performance is important. For some, it is a learned behavior and not instinctual. If you stagnate a child with one person for years on end, they never learn how to adapt to a change in leadership. Change is part of the life experience. By limiting change, you are not preparing your child for the future.

The Neurologist

At the beginning of this school year, we had our appointment to meet with the new neurologist. The nurse practitioner in the intake interview was a little disgruntled that we didn't have a referral from a physician. (We ignored the attitude.) Both the nurse practitioner and the neurologist evaluated our son. They also asked us the same questions that had been asked over and over again by other providers regarding what behaviors we had noticed, when milestones were achieved in development, etc. We discovered that writing down early childhood milestones when they occurred was very helpful. Relying on your memory alone can be frustrating when you are speaking with a medical provider. If you notice particular behaviors that do not seem typical, write them down with your child's age and dates. It's much easier to look back on what you wrote than to have to rely on your memory. Keeping a binder is particularly helpful. In our binder were notes, doctor and medical reports, etc., so that everything was all in one place, logically organized, and easily accessible. I carried my binder to every doctor appointment and Child Study Team meeting for many years.

Once the questions were finished, the doctor came in and performed a series of physical tests as well as mental ones that didn't seem all that extensive to us. Our son's initial evaluation took a full day at the first children's hospital. Sometimes our son would do what he was asked to do. Other times, he would refuse outright. At the end of the visit, the nurse practitioner very gently informed us that our child was autistic. We could tell she was trying to be sensitive with us about the diagnosis. We laughed a bit and told her she didn't have to worry about how we would react - we knew our son was autistic, and we were just there to get a formal diagnosis. An MRI and an EEG were requested and scheduled along with a follow-up appointment with the doctor to discuss the results. Fifteen years ago, this was standard procedure when you went to a neurologist to have an official diagnosis. It's not anymore. (There are several articles about autistic brain structure, functions, and studies on the website of Spectrumnews.org if you are interested in additional reading.)

The MRI

Since our son couldn't sit still, he would be given anesthesia so he would sleep through the MRI procedure. That meant that he would have to have an IV - a scary prospect and my usual anxiety about a procedure began. I speak about my anxiety quite a bit here for a good reason. The general anxiety of being a parent with a typical child is bad enough: the anxiety I feel raising a child with special needs never lets me relax. Do you feel like you are always waiting for the next bomb to drop and at the same time trying to avoid it? I do not know whether we just get used to the stress or the anxiety actually decreases as our child ages, but things do seem to get more manageable as our child grows.

During the MRI visit, they gave him liquid medication to relax him before they put in the IV line. We had brought with us a mini DVD player so he would have something to do while he waited. Very soon he couldn't focus and he told his father "I see two of you, Daddy." He was happy and relaxed. The IV went in with no problem and soon he was snoozing away. Afterward, he took a while to wake up from the anesthesia; and he had some intense nausea associated with it. The drive home was not pleasant, but the medication they gave him kept him from being sick in the car. There was a bag ready just in case: by now, we had enough experience with vomiting and knew how to be prepared.

The EEG

The EEG was different. We were told to wake him in the early hours of the morning (think 2:00 a.m.) and keep him awake until we got to the office for an early morning visit. We took turns keeping him awake. For the drive to the office, a small building block kit he could put together on the way was used to keep him occupied. The drive was thirty minutes; he would need help from me to build his kit. I was so car sick from trying to read the directions and help him build the toy that I wanted to kiss the ground when we got there. Fortunately, our son did not get car sick, so he was just fine. Although he was quite sleepy, we had kept him awake, as directed.

They glued electrodes all over his head and let him lie down. I worried about how he was going to deal with this strange new event in his life, but he was so tired that he didn't care about the 'stuff' that was glued to his head and fell asleep almost immediately. They would wake him periodically, and he would just blink at them and then go back to sleep. If you didn't count the whole 'trying to keep him awake" time, the process was a relatively easy procedure.

After the tests, we went back to the neurologist for our follow-up visit. The doctor confirmed the diagnosis and said something to us that has stayed with me. He said, "Your son is going to be fine. You'll just have to get him through school." All these years, I have held on to that statement. This physician gave me considerable hope for our son's future, especially when things became difficult due to his disability in his younger years. Each time our son conquers a milestone, I am reminded of what this doctor said to us. So far, he has been right. We are not finished with the whole school experience and adjustment to adult life; however, because of what he said, the future isn't quite as scary as it seemed at the beginning.

Kindergarten

Our son continued to adjust to going to school full-time. Some days, of course, were more difficult than others. We continued with the behavior supports that were developed in pre-school and added new ones recommended by his therapists. His teacher continued with the logbook entries. Looking back at it, our son showed significant growth that year. He conquered the chaos of the "all-purpose" room, where they would have the students sit on the floor for assemblies. He stopped fighting the clean-up process after snack time and began to eat more regularly. Hitting was still a major issue in the beginning, but by the end of Kindergarten, it was mostly resolved. He learned to reach out to his teacher if he had a problem with another student instead of lashing out in anger with his fists. In December, he sang with his classmates at our local tree-lighting ceremony. I took a picture of him with his teacher that night and gave her a copy. She kept that photo on her desk for many years. Of course, he still had issues, but there was real growth and that was such a relief to me!

Another form of relief for me was the "mom break." I was so tired and beyond ready for a little "me" time! Taking care of a special needs individual is exhausting. Acknowledging that fact doesn't mean you do not love that person. Everyone needs to have time to relax and unwind from life's daily stresses. For a little while, I didn't know what to do with myself. I joined a weight loss program and started walking with some friends four times a week for an hour all year long. When the weather wasn't nice enough outside, we would walk the local indoor mall, which had a special time designated before the stores opened for mall walkers. Doing something that didn't involve my child for a change was really good for me. This is important for everyone! Taking time for myself made me a better parent and more patient with our son during those tough times.

Volunteering was still very important to me. Being a room mom meant the added responsibility of putting together parties and events that took place in kindergarten but also enabled me to be in the classroom to observe our son at these events. Volunteering as room mom also paved the way for me to actively enter the classroom to read or do small projects associated with the holidays with all the children. The class was small, but the teacher was more than happy for another set of hands to assist. She made me feel part of the class and let me know, as in previous years, if an evening follow-through was necessary regarding trouble our son had during the school day.

During this time, I was fortunate enough to be able to stay at home with our son for his formative years. I know that many of you have to work: you do not have a choice. While frustrating, you can still work with your child in the evenings, early mornings, and on the weekends. I make this suggestion to you because this is what we did when it was time for me to return to work. This double duty is definitely exhausting. Be proactive - ask and teach others to help you. Your significant other can take a turn. Is there another adult family member you are living with that can help lift some of the burdens on you? Inform your child's daycare or after-school program about certain strategies you use at home that work well. Reach out to your child's grandparents, aunts, and uncles. Teach them what to do. They may be afraid at first, but be understanding regarding their fear. Let them know you will start small (an hour for the first time) and that you will be there if they need to call you or come back to pick your child up. Even better, ask them to come to your house for a bit to give you a break. Tell them you need help. There is no shame in this! There is no need for you to shoulder this burden alone and you shouldn't have to be the only one responsible for continuous care at all times. Make those around you understand how important this is to your well-being and that of your child. If you still can't get help from them, contact your local autism center. My center paid for a provider/caregiver to watch a child for a few hours to give the parent a break every week. Asking for help from those around you is not a weakness. Raising an autistic child requires you to be strong and self-care is an important tool for you to stay strong.

Summer

During the last few weeks of the kindergarten year, our son's behavior unexpectedly began to deteriorate in class. The teacher called me in to observe him because she was perplexed. Had we given him any new foods? Has anything changed at home? Everything was the same. His behavior was really odd. Refusals had become a considerable problem. He wouldn't focus on me when his name was called and all he wanted to do was play with the toys away from his desk. He had retreated into his own little world. The only possible cause we could think of was that she had begun to talk about first grade and having a new teacher. I'm sure she told the students that they had to behave a certain way as first graders. It's important to prepare them for the upcoming change. Since this was in the last few weeks of school, I really didn't worry about it. We both figured he was apprehensive about a new teacher and excited about having summer off from school.

The summer before first grade we continued to visit the Sensory Playhouse, and he also attended a class at the local library. Because leaving still wasn't an option for me, I read a book nearby. He did moderately well in the class. He wasn't a model student, but every time he finished a project, we celebrated. Please note, it is not helpful for you to compare your son or daughter with other children, even if they are in the same classroom setting. This is a hard lesson to learn; but, trust me, comparisons never make you feel better. Your child is different. If you want to compare their behavior to one of their prior visits, that's okay. I personally like to have each visit be a fresh start, a new chance for the child to work hard and do their best.

That summer, we also became more comfortable with traveling. We went on trips as a family and often would go to the beach for mom-and-son time. I love to travel and was so excited when he adapted to travel more easily than before. We went to Walt Disney World and SeaWorld with my parents. Since this was in October during his kindergarten year, we asked his teacher for any homework he would miss. She said to have him draw a picture and write one or two simple sentences about what he did each day. For most kids, this is a really easy assignment. For a young man who doesn't like to draw or color and absolutely hates writing, this was a difficult project. Still, we didn't back down from this difficult task. Since we would get home late at night, and he would be tired at the end of the day, each morning after breakfast before we headed out, he did his page from the prior day. Being able to go to the next fun adventure was a reward for doing the page. If he didn't do his page, we couldn't leave. We ended up with a really cute book at the end. I still have it.

Traveling and Vacations

How did we successfully travel with our Autistic son and have an enjoyable time as a family? First, please accept you can't expect your child to always entertain themselves. So many people just drag their kids somewhere and do not make any effort to give them things to entertain them should they become bored! Then, those same parents become upset when the child acts up. (Guess what mom and dad? Boredom sucks!) Also, a child with autism can be very specific about what they consider to be fun and what is not! To cut down on boredom and tantrums, we did many varied activities. Of course, we still experienced negative behaviors at times, but with forethought and planning, those instances were few and far between.

One year, we asked for a miniature DVD player to receive as a gift. Once we had it, we never traveled without it. If we were going to be in the car or on a plane for a long period of time, I would pick up a new DVD or two to keep him occupied for the drive or flight. You can also rent DVDs at a local library if you can't afford something new. These days, another option is downloading movies onto your devices. The possibilities for entertainment are quite limitless!

In addition to movies, I would purchase a few new small toys and hide them in our suitcase. During downtime on vacation when he would get bored, because you can't be busy non-stop, he would become excited about receiving something new. A new toy was worth hours of play! They also make great rewards for good behavior. We were able to afford to purchase these items because at Christmas some of my relatives would send us all gift cards. I would hold on to them and use them right before we would go on a trip to purchase new and interesting things.

Along with the new toys, we had a small backpack full of items he liked. This little backpack went everywhere with us. Our son was old enough to help choose what he wanted to bring with him. The only limits were that the toys had to fit in the backpack and he had to be the one to carry it. This was his responsibility. This bag of toys kept him occupied and gave us activities to do with him if he didn't want to play by himself. The toy bag also served as a way to meet other children and develop those important socialization skills. Whip out a bag of toys and any child within a twenty-foot radius will gravitate to you. Do yourself a favor and get a little backpack for your child. You will be able to take him or her anywhere and not worry so much about them getting into something they shouldn't.

We found that sticking to a routine, even on vacation, helped keep meltdowns to a minimum. Every night we still played the same music CD at bedtime. We kept to the same bedtime routine we had at home. We always had squishes, read before bed, and went to bed at 9:00 p.m. Keeping to this schedule gave our son a sense of security in a new environment.

When planning your vacation, be sure to include some things that your child is interested in doing. I'm not saying plan your entire vacation around your child. Interspersing things they enjoy with things that might not interest them as much, gives your child incentive to look forward to something during those times that are not so thrilling. This also helps your child understand that vacation is for everyone, which means everyone gets a chance to do something they like at one time or another.

When our son got a little older, we added a handheld device. I forget how old he was when we gave him his first handheld gaming device. (I'm still on the fence about if this was good or bad.) Our son loves video games. The games occupied him no matter where we went. The device also served as a socialization tool, because other children would be interested in what he was doing. He would happily sit with them and play while he explained to them what was going on in the game. However, he did use this device as a crutch when he was uncomfortable in a social situation even when he was older. Now that he has switched over to a cell phone, we still need to remind him at times that it is more important to talk with family or friends at a party. The older he gets, the more he understands and has been able to set the phone aside or leave any device in the car if necessary.

One final note regarding vacations. It is extremely hard for an autistic person to go non-stop and be stuck in a room with people all the time. While we cherish our downtime, they need to have quiet, private time to unwind and not worry about being social. Build this into your vacation routine. Our vacations now consist of going to breakfast, spending the morning and early afternoon doing an activity and having lunch out, then returning to the room for several hours of downtime before going out in the evening for dinner and any entertainment. At first, having this kind of routine on vacation felt odd to me. Now, I treasure it.

Kindergarten and the summer after was a pivotal year for our son. The time was full of growth and discovery - for him and for us. It is still one of my favorite years. In retrospect, this was the year when I began to understand that time moves on despite our difficulties, and, with time, growth and joy happen. The experience may not be quite what we expect or as much as we would like; but even with difficulties, there will be golden moments where your child - and you - will thrive.

Chapter 8

The IEP Or The 504

I f your child is entering the public school system, you will be having a discussion about creating an Individualized Education Program (IEP) or 504 Plan for them. Sometimes you have to make a choice or a choice is made for you because you feel others are more knowledgeable about what will work best for your child. Understanding the difference between an IEP and a 504 Plan can be overwhelming at first. Understood.org has a chart and article entitled "*The Differences Between IEPs and 504 Plans.*" This site has excellent information and other links that are helpful. This isn't the only website that offers this information. If you do an Internet search, many sites pop up.

As a clarification, some of the specifics in this chapter pertain to the special education laws in New Jersey. This is because this is where our son was raised. Each state's laws are different, so you will want to make sure you do some research about the specific guidelines where you live.

When I was faced with trying to figure out the difference between an IEP and a 504 Plan, information was not as easily accessible. Our son's early intervention therapist explained this to me in oversimplified terms, but this still helped guide me when I was asked, "Do you want to switch to a 504 Plan?"

Simply put, you use an IEP when your child is still in the stages of needing a set plan and special services to grow educationally. The IEP lists goals to achieve each year, not just from your child's therapists but from the school social worker or psychologist and your child's teacher. The IEP grows with your child and is an in-depth document of what your child needs to continue to do to make progress and grow in the educational setting.

Recently, I had a conversation with someone I consider a specialist regarding the IEP and the 504 in New Jersey. She clarified the main difference between the two. The type of modification that is being offered is what makes the difference. If your child is classified and has a learning disability and or speech delay, then you are looking at an IEP. The reason is that they may need modifications requiring changes to the curriculum requirements. For example, you may see goals for reading levels or content area comprehension. If your child is classified and has no learning disability requiring changes to the educational/curriculum guidelines, then you are looking at a 504 Plan. She informed me that you can still get OT and PT with a 504 Plan. However, speech therapy is different. It has its own set of IEP requirements. In New Jersey, you can have a 504 Plan and a Speech IEP at the same time.

So, first, you have to qualify for an IEP. For the sake of argument let's say your child receives an ASD classification (through a diagnosis) and, therefore, requires learning adjustments due to learning delays. You are looking at an IEP. However, several years into your child's education you may be told to switch to a 504 Plan. Years ago, I remember having a conversation with a fellow parent who was upset that her Child Study Team suggested that she should switch to a 504 Plan because her son was doing so well in school. We joked and said, "Are you telling me my son is suddenly not autistic anymore?" At the time, we really didn't understand the difference.

The criteria for a 504 Plan qualification are less stringent than for that of an IEP. Your child may need services or help with certain areas due to their disability, but there is no plan for the growth of learning skills. You can have a 504 Plan because your child has a peanut allergy. You can have a 504 Plan that states your child needs extended time to test or turn in homework assignments. It is not going to say, "Our goal for this year is for Johnny to increase his reading level by one grade level." A 504 Plan could say, "Johnny is unable to tie his shoes due to musculature issues; and, therefore, will require the assistance of an aide to do so," or it can say, "Johnny will receive OT one time a week to help with fine motor skills." It could even include both of these statements.

We started with an IEP. Our son had a lot of growing to do, and he needed therapy to achieve it in many areas. At three he was non-verbal. He also needed behavioral support in the classroom and help with educational goals. He required speech therapy, occupational therapy, help socializing with his peers, and, of course, help with things like learning the alphabet and learning to form letters. When we had our son re-evaluated for Asperger's Syndrome and ADHD in the fifth grade, the neuropsychologist commented that our IEP was one of the best she had ever seen. We have been fortunate. Since our school district shared services with what would one day be our son's middle and high school district, his IEP would carry that format into later years.

We were never told that we needed to change to a 504 Plan. This is not the case for everyone: sometimes it is not just a recommendation. If you find yourself in that type of situation, do what you always do: research, talk to people, be open to suggestions, and remember, you can always update your child's 504 Plan as necessary if you find that something is not working. Our son had an IEP up until the eleventh grade. He was released from speech therapy after sixth grade and occupational therapy after eighth grade.

I really liked our IEP and its format. However, at the end of tenth grade a special education teacher and our school psychologist mentioned that if our son wanted support in college, it would be much easier to obtain them if he already had a 504 Plan in place. A 504 Plan will travel with your son or daughter to college; an IEP does not. Thinking ahead and with the sage advice of a disabled person who had been there herself, we switched to a 504 Plan.

Currently, I am not enamored with our 504 Plan. This is something for me to revisit for his future. To me, the plan seems too vague and open to interpretation perhaps because it was created for a high school environment and not college. In high school, on occasion speaking with a teacher was necessary to gently remind them about some supports and considerations that are listed. Sometimes, I get a nagging and terrible feeling that they never bothered to read his 504 Plan. However, there is no argument that our son no longer needs an IEP. He needs extended deadlines for handing things in, notes if possible, and extended time for testing. For that, the 504 Plan did its job in high school.

More Specifics

The IEP and 504 Plan originate from different laws. However, they can overlap in related services, which is why parents often get confused. The goal of a 504 Plan is to prevent discrimination against individuals with disabilities and stems from Section 504 of the Rehabilitation Act of 1973.

A 504 Plan adjusts a person's environment in response to their particular needs. Equal access to education or employment is its main purpose. Unlike an IEP, there is no law that requires a 504 Plan to be re-evaluated every year. A child or adult may need accommodations so that they can continue in school or at their job without being discriminated against. An example that is often used is if your child has a peanut allergy. At lunch, their 504 Plan will have accommodations regarding a separate table where the child can sit with some peers but will not be exposed to peanuts. They still get to have lunch with their peers, but they just can't sit at a table where they could be exposed to peanut products for their own safety.

The IEP (which stands for Individualized Education Plan) originates from the Individuals with Disabilities Education Act (IDEA). Some key points regarding an IEP are as follows here (as interpreted by New Jersey law):

- Disabled children should be provided with an education that is created to meet their unique needs in the least restrictive environment.

- It requires a specific diagnosis, which the school will use as a classification. At this time there are thirteen different categories, and autism (ASD) is one of them. However, even if you have a classification such as ASD, you still will need to show that your child's disability hampers their ability to succeed educationally in their current school environment.

- The IEP must be reviewed and "created" every school year.

- The guidelines for an IEP have strict timelines and procedures that must be followed by federal law.

Questions If You're Unhappy

I am actually glad that we did start with a 504 Plan in eleventh grade. This gave me additional time to evaluate what worked, and what didn't, during that school year so adjustments could be made for his senior year. For instance, due to long-term virtual learning because of COVID-19, a paragraph was added to the document addressing the unique problems our son has with this type of learning style and requested certain accommodations to help him.

So what do you do if you feel your IEP is lacking? If you feel that your school's Child Study Team is unable to create a better IEP for your child, perhaps you can enlist the services of your neuropsychologist. Ours said she often offers to work with schools and parents to put together an IEP that better meets the needs of a student. I found a resource article on Complexchild.org that offers a great deal of information for a parent in need of help or guidance.

Generally, an IEP may have sections on learning environments; recommendations for the coming school year and learning modification and goals; special equipment considerations; speech, occupational or physical therapy plans; and, if needed, discipline modifications. These are only a few examples of what an IEP may contain. Depending on your school and the state you live in, yours will be unique to your child.

In New Jersey, you do not have to sign off on the IEP on the date you receive it. You can tell them you would like to take the draft IEP home and read the document over again when you have more time. However, be aware that there are laws that state if you do not sign off on the IEP or send a letter stating that you need to meet again or are requesting mediation, then within a certain number of days that IEP is considered implemented without your signature. Watch your timelines.

Those of you who are already familiar with the public school system and IEPs may notice that I have not talked about the need for mediation. That is because we never needed it. For some, unfortunately, that is not the case. If you are at the point where no one can agree on services and implementation of them, then it may be time for an outside arbitrator.

Our Child Study Team provided us each year with a book explaining a child's special education rights (again in New Jersey). This book contained deadlines, explanations, and procedures. I read through ours in the early years (not all at once) when unsure of a deadline or how to go forward with a given challenge. Mediation instructions are found in that book.

If we had ever needed to go through the mediation process, we probably would have, at the very least, chosen an advocate who had experience with the system. Knowing when to ask for help from an expert is just as important as doing things yourself. Do not feel like you need to know everything. Asking for help is okay. Not sure where to ask? Start with your local autism center or do an Internet search for help with IEPs in your state. A word of advice here: make sure you and your advocate are on the same page about your child's needs and what you want to present. You don't want to get to the mediation table and find out that your goals and theirs are not the same.

What Type of School

Finally, it is important to note that our son attended school in the public school system and was considered high-functioning. Some school districts may need to send your child to a specialized school because they can not provide the services that your child may require. Also, if your child is attending a charter school or private school, things may be different. Commonwealth Learning Center has a web page that provides excellent information about this difference.

Before you decide the grass is greener on the other side of the hill, make sure you do some significant research and ask your potential target school questions specifically pertaining to your child and to your circumstance. A private school may be a better fit for your child - or it may not. It's up to you to decide.

Chapter 9

Your Marriage - Holding Things Together

This was one of the more difficult chapters for me to write. Once done, my husband read not just this chapter but the entire book. This thrilled me as he has never read a book about autism. He refused to read anything about autism for many years. To my knowledge, my book is the only one he has read to date. His only comment was that I glossed over how he made things difficult at times and how much we argued. This chapter is now the revised version, giving you some of our hard and honest truths.

How cool is it that my husband told me to tell the world he was "pretty much a jerk" in the early years of raising our son? His understanding of autism, and of himself, has grown considerably since that time. I have come to appreciate his point of view more, as well. In case you are wondering - yes, we still argue over what we feel is the best course to take with our son. We always will. His expectations for our son are the same as if our son was a typical child. He knows he's autistic, but he doesn't care. He will tell you that. His goal is to get this kid independent and out of the house. It's his only goal.

His perspective is drastically different from mine. Different doesn't mean less valuable. My husband commented a time or two that it's pointless to argue with me when a decision has to be made regarding our son's care. He's right. I fully admit to being obstinate about what should or shouldn't be done to help our son. However, it's always after a great deal of research on the topic of discussion that enables me to stand my ground. Either that or it's going to be more work for me doing things the way he suggests, and I'm often just not up to it.

As I mentioned before, he had never picked up a book about autism until he read mine. He didn't even realize that our son was autistic until our son was about seven years old: we visited an autism center to see what services we could get for our son. My husband fought with me the whole drive there. "Why do we need to go here? I don't do counseling." Then after meeting with the staff, he said, "Our son is autistic?" Where had my husband been all these years? He said he knew our son had Asperger's Syndrome but didn't think that was autism.

Our Experience

Early in our marriage, although we both liked children, we had no plans to have any. Once my husband graduated from college, we lived for a few years with his mom to save for a down payment on a house. Once in a house, I began to push hard to have a child.

Being an optimist, I ignored our problem of getting pregnant for a while. Once two years passed, though, I began to pressure him to investigate why we were having a problem. Usually, doctors start with the gentleman first. That means an evaluation of his "swimmers" - a sperm check. That "test," which you have to submit two separate times, was embarrassing for my husband but he did this anyway. When the results came back, medication was recommended for him. He was game, only because of me.

He lasted three months on the medication. The drug made him crazy, and he finally stopped taking it without telling me because he just couldn't handle it anymore. He was trying to figure out how to tell me when our positive pregnancy test result came back. (He didn't have to tell me about stopping the medication, but he did.) He's that kind of guy. Our marriage is that kind of marriage. He loves me so much that he was willing to step out of his comfort zone to give me a child.

But to be blunt, he was terrified and didn't have any confidence in himself as a dad. My focus was completely on having a child, and I missed his apprehensions.

Once pregnant, we had an amniocentesis to rule out chromosomal abnormalities. This was important to him, not so much to me. I had to compromise somewhere. The test came back normal. Autism never entered our minds. In 2002, via c-section, a beautiful baby boy was born. He was not little, and we felt like we went home with a three-month-old, not a newborn. Aside from the milk protein problem explained in an earlier chapter, things were mostly normal.

My husband didn't have a problem with me choosing to be a stay-at-home mom. He had an odd work schedule because he worked in retail and would help me if asked when he was home. However, if I asked, there was always a lot of complaining that came with it. In addition, he wouldn't listen to me about how he should do whatever needed to be done when it came to our son. He wanted to do things his way if he was being forced to help. This meant that our child would struggle because of my husband's lack of understanding, and without intervention, this wasn't going to be a good experience for either one of them.

When I discovered autism was a real possibility, I didn't know how to tell him. He had been very vocal about not being the type of parent who could deal with a child who required special needs before our pregnancy. Somehow, we managed to communicate; and my role as his wife changed. My focus changed upon becoming a mother. That changed even more after finding out that our son was different. For a time, I no longer concentrated on our marriage. Instead, my focus was on helping our son as much as possible. I voraciously read anything about sensory issues and by extension autism. Once early intervention started for our son, his learning and therapies consumed our lives. On the days my husband was home from work, he stayed with us and participated in the sessions a little bit. While he was kind to our therapist, he didn't always agree with some of the therapy and made sure to tell me so.

He didn't know what to do, so he stepped back and let me take care of things, and felt he was there to support me in his own way. At least that is how things started. As time passed, he didn't (and still doesn't) want to treat our son any differently than if he was raising a typical child. If asked to take us to a doctor's visit, he would, but would argue with me about the necessity of seeing a particular doctor beforehand and all the way to the doctor's office. This argument would always include me defending why we needed to go for that particular therapy or to see that physician.

My time was spent on learning to cope with the stress of raising a child with special needs, and rarely did I request help. There was no energy or patience left for all the effort to explain how and why we should do something. At the time, he didn't want to hear my reasons anyway. The only thing we argued about was how to take care of our son.

To head off the arguments as much as possible, I just did every-thing. My thinking was he worked hard and should have time to rest on his days off. In retrospect, should I have shouldered that burden completely? It's always easier to look back and see things from a different perspective. Perhaps pushing him to put our son to bed on the days he was off, every day he was off, would have helped him to develop a better relationship with our son. Would forcing him to play with our son using the techniques taught by the therapists have worked? Would he have resented me if made to attend therapy groups and read books on autism? Knowing him, quite possibly, yes. Also, there was a real possibility that if pushed too hard, he would just say "I can't." Not, "No," but more of "I can't handle this." Although often tired from being our son's sole caregiver all day, it kept me from having to argue with my husband about how to take care of our son. Making him feel terrible and "less" because he couldn't help was not constructive for any of us.

I'll never know for sure if pushing more would have helped our relationship or hurt it. My husband tells me he was so tired from the stress of work that he didn't want to help. So that alone might have led to some serious arguments. Plus, of course, he would want to do things his way. For example our bedtime routine: at the same time every night, we would head upstairs (often with a bit of argument from our son). Then I would brush his teeth, help him get dressed for bed, do joint compression, and read stories. In the early years, lying down in bed with our son until he fell asleep was common. You can imagine how my husband felt about all of that! Most nights, I would wander into our bedroom and go right to sleep myself - leaving us no alone time and often not even saying good night.

Sharing The Responsibility

Despite all the reasons for avoiding the "tough path," guilty feelings of having deprived him of forming a better relationship with our son still haunt me. The importance of reaching out to your significant other and sharing the burden of responsibility can't be stressed enough.

How do you do this? My first suggestion is that you read books, and blogs, and search websites for information *together*. Even if you have to take turns reading to each other aloud, make this a commitment to each other to work together to learn as much as possible about ASD. If you look up something on the internet, show it to your spouse. Have them read what you found and then discuss how you feel about what was read.

Together, learn all the therapies that will help your child. If that is not possible, show your spouse how to do therapy until they are comfortable with it. Let them take care of that awesome child you both created, more than just once in a while when you need a break. Shouldering the burden can help form a stronger bond than if one person alone is taking care of everything.

I'm afraid that I gave the impression to my husband that he couldn't take care of our son properly in the early years. This undermined his confidence in being a father. If we had been in therapy, the therapist would have told him that he needed to do more with our son. That person would have told me to be less rigid about handing over the responsibilities

Each of you will have different strengths and weaknesses depending on how you interact with your child. My husband is far better at pushing our son beyond his comfort zone. This took me years to understand. I should have relied on that skill. You both need to figure out each other's strengths and discuss how best to use them for everyone's benefit. Likewise, do not be afraid to discuss your weaknesses. But, do not call them that! Just like some people are better at sports or math, let your significant other know that you think they are competent, and possibly better, at handling a situation.

Can you sense a theme in all my suggestions? Communication is critically important in a marriage. Not just any communication, but kind and thoughtful communication. If you see that your significant other is struggling with a certain task and feel you could do it better, please resist the need to jump in and "help." At a different time, other than when they are struggling, offer some suggestions that could help them (if they are open to it) or read together some research you already found regarding the issue. You are both in this together, treat each other kindly, always. Of course, being human, you are still going to argue about things. There is no way to avoid that. What I'm suggesting is that you learn to argue *constructively*.

In all the years that we have been together raising this amazing son, never once was divorce a consideration for us. I got angry, cried, raged, stopped talking, and more, but I considered that part of a normal marriage. He's not perfect and neither am I. Why should our marriage be any different?

Statistics on Divorce

When you're raising a child with special needs, the conversation eventually comes up with your peers regarding the rate of divorce due to stress. It's possible that you are curious about the statistical data on the divorce rate of parents raising a child with ASD, as opposed to those that are raising a neurotypical child. Thinking it would be interesting and helpful, I began to research what studies have been done to find an answer to that question. This was extremely frustrating. Here is a brief summary of what my research uncovered.

The first thing that jumps out at you when you start to do an internet search regarding this topic is the 80% statistic of the divorce rate for parents raising a child with ASD. There was an overwhelming majority of research debunking that percentage in almost every article and paper I found. Just like these researchers, I tried to find where this 80% figure came from and couldn't.

That's good, right? Well, this certainly made me feel better. Simply put, the 80% figure is not true.

I can hear your protests right now. You're saying, "Wait a minute! My marriage has really suffered from the stress of raising a child on the spectrum!" The struggle is real. Let's look a bit deeper and see what percentages other studies found.

Many of the articles I found referenced a study printed in the Journal of Family Psychology. *The Relative Risk And Timing of Divorce in Families of Children With An Autism Spectrum Disorder.* The study involved approximately 782 families, half of which were raising at least one child with autism. The other half were raising neurotypical children. I really liked this study because it was extremely detailed in its empirical data. The study took into account the ages of the mother and child, ethnicity, education, biological or adoptive child, timing of the divorce, and more.

In summary, they found that parents raising a child with ASD were about ten percent more likely to divorce than the control group of parents who did not. It also found that the stress for married couples, while leveling off and easing up in the neurotypical child group around age eight, continued for the group with an ASD child all the way through to young adulthood. This at least appears to be more reflective of what we see in real life.

Another article from the Interactive Autism Network published on April 11, 2017, by Marina Sarris called, *Under A Looking Glass: What's the Truth About Autism and Marriage*, referred to a study conducted by researchers from both the Kennedy Krieger Institute and Johns Hopkins University. Unlike the above study by Hartley, et al., which only took into account two states, this study was nationwide and encompassed almost 78,000 parents. Of this number, 913 of them were raising a child with ASD. This study found that:

"After controlling for relevant covariates, results from multivariate analyses revealed no evidence to suggest that children with ASD are at an increased risk for living in a household not comprised of their two biological or adoptive parents compared to children without ASD in the United States."

The study also mentions why its findings were different from those of the well-known Hartley, et al, 2010, study. One interesting conclusion was it didn't matter if the child was high functioning or more impaired on the spectrum.

There is no simple answer to this question. However, the 80% number is just a myth. More exploration and study are needed on the subject. Instead of focusing on statistics, I think it's more important to focus on what makes any marriage successful.

Go ahead and do an Internet search for traits of a successful marriage and see what pops up! Communication, trust, humor, forgiveness, teamwork, and empathy are only a few of the positive traits suggested by therapists. Anyone who has been married for a while will tell you that keeping a marriage together is hard work. Getting married is easy - staying married is hard!

At the time this chapter was written, we had recently celebrated our thirty-first wedding anniversary. To me, marriage is like a ride on a roller coaster. There are times that are exhilarating and awesome like when you're rushing down that great big hill. There are other times too when you are struggling with everything you have to just hold it all together as you creep slowly back up to the top of that peak in anticipation of the next thrilling moment.

If you are struggling right now with your marriage due to the extensive stress of raising a child with ASD, know that you are not alone. I recommend very much that both of you attend a support group and, if needed, a marriage counselor. A marriage counselor is not going to tell you there is no hope for your marriage and that you might as well divorce. A good one will provide strategies that you probably never even thought about to help you stay connected with your significant other. It's not a stigma or a poor reflection of your marriage to seek out professional help.

Maintaining your marriage is just as important as learning and helping your ASD child. Do not let your marriage take a back seat. Just as you will fight to give the best to your child, fight to give the best to your marriage and each other.

Sadly, some of you who are reading this right now didn't have the option of working together to keep your marriage viable. A successful marriage takes two people working together toward the same goal. You both have to want the same thing. If one partner doesn't want to put the time and work into having a loving relationship that includes your autistic child, then you may have (or have had) a hard decision to make. If they won't seek counseling with you, I still encourage you to go yourself. Please be assured that you may feel like you are alone, but you are not. Help is out there. You only need to reach for help and be open to receiving it.

Chapter 10

Keeping Your Sense of Humor and Joy

I s there anything better than laughter at making us feel better? That, with a good healthy dose of optimism, gets me through most situations. I am a supremely optimistic person and try to see the silver lining in every cloud. I like my blinders and my rose-colored glasses and do not look for problems. Trouble will find me soon enough, to my way of thinking. Worrying about negative things that can happen ahead of time is not constructive. Sure, when it comes to our safety sometimes we do have to think about negative consequences, but that's not quite the same thing.

When a difficult situation arises, I look for ways to cope with humor. My parents can take partial credit for this, I'm sure. There were quite a few difficulties we got through using our sense of humor to buffer a tough life experience while growing up. Life is full of tough experiences, but it's also full of joyous moments and lots of humor too! The trick is that you have to look for and recognize them.

If you are like me, it's easy to remember and dwell on the difficult times. It's also easy to get bogged down with anxiety when you do so. Humor is a wonderful way to cope. To be clear, we made sure our son never felt like we were laughing at him. We laugh with him if possible, but never make fun of him as part of our humor. That's just mean and can be devastating to an autistic child.

I do not want you to think after reading this book that my life has been awful just because we have had some challenges. Honestly, keeping our sense of humor helped us get through many difficult situations. This is what helps me keep my sanity. Here are a few stories from the early years that are good examples of using humor to cope. Enjoy, and do not forget to smile and laugh!

The Dog and The Dog Bone

Our dog was about three when we brought our son home from the hospital. She was not impressed. She was a mite pissed. I noticed that she wasn't listening to me right before we found out about being pregnant. That big girl (a black lab) knew before we did that her world was going to change. She adjusted.

One day when our son was about twelve months old, I walked into the kitchen looking to find where he had wandered while I was out of earshot. All the cabinets in the kitchen had child locks on them. All but one. The cabinet was on the lower level and held my crock pot, mixer, and the box of large dog bones right up front. Our son, who is a really picky eater, had opened the cabinet, pulled out a great big bone, sat down, and proceeded to gnaw away on it. Our dog looked at me like "What the hell!" Of course, I couldn't just take the bone from our son. First, a picture needed to be captured. It's one of my favorite pictures and makes me smile every time the book gets brought out. He's so happy he found his treat and has a giant smile on his face. It's a picture full of joy.

Another time when he was about three and a half years old or so, I walked out into the living room to find him straddling the dog, who was sitting nicely on her hind legs. He had his hands on her soft ears and was twisting them like he was revving a motorcycle, noises included. Ok, so we do not have a picture of that one. Our dog was patient with him, but that only went so far. I quickly told him he shouldn't do that because he could hurt her and distracted him with something else. But for one second, I just stood there watching and laughing. The look of resignation on the poor dog's face was so funny. Such a typical thing for a kid to do from our nontypical son.

Photo Shoots

My cell phone camera didn't take very good pictures. When our son was small, my husband bought me a cute little digital camera. This little neon green camera went everywhere with us. To me, every opportunity to take a snapshot of life is a gift. Time goes by so fast and memories can fade. Sometimes remembering a beautiful moment requires the reminder of a photograph. For me, they are quick little pick-me-ups that make me smile. For our son, they are important reminders of things he doesn't remember.

I can remember quite a few "photo sessions" that were great fun with our son. These aren't the kind that you pose for but more spontaneous moments in time. For example, one day the cleanly washed cover for the couch was on the floor waiting for me to put it back on. Our son was learning to get around and loved to explore. Using the couch cover, we had a short session of peek-a-boo. He was smiling so brightly and laughing so hard that I immediately brought out the camera and began to take pictures. We had such fun that day and, again, the photo from that "session" is one of my favorite pictures. There is a copy on my desk at work, as a reminder of the happy spontaneous play session.

The First Birthday Party and Cake

I made our son a smash cake for his first birthday. The cake was vanilla with chocolate icing. (Because what kid doesn't like chocolate?) Our kid. He wanted nothing to do with it. Finally, in desperation, I smudged some icing on his fingers and face and snapped a quick picture. Good grief, what a "mean mom" moment. He screamed his head off. He really didn't like sweet things.

That was the only difficulty during the party. While it was stressful having a large group of people in our house, his first birthday party was an enjoyable experience. Once shown how to open his gifts, our son loved ripping the paper. His favorite gift was a stuffed rocking horse my parents gave him. I think he smiled for hours that day. The cake part was insignificant. Looking back, I remember the joy on his face and his adorable look of concentration as he began to unwrap a gift for the first time.

The Puking - Oh God the Puking!

The annual stomach virus that most parents experience with their preschool children was not a stranger in our house. If anything, the virus visited us so often, I wondered if we would ever not have a time that didn't involve getting the stomach bug at least two or more times a year.

It seems our son has "christened" more parts of the house than most children, although that is probably not really the case. However, it is true that up until this past year, my husband has never owned a car that our son hasn't vomited in.

The first two years of preschool were particularly grueling. He brought home every sickness he was exposed to by his peers. After suffering through the sickness himself, he would give it to me. My resistance built up during those years as well. This was before COVID, masks, etc.

So how is vomiting funny? Well, our son would try to run away from the actual act of throwing up. Picture this, a cute toddler in nothing but his diaper sitting on the couch watching one of his favorite programs. Completely out of the blue, he upchucks. No warning, just puke all over the couch, the rug, and himself. The crying begins. Cleaning him up first, he settles down to watch more of the DVD in another chair that is currently clean. After scrubbing the mess on the couch and rug, I brought in a trash pail because I am an optimist and hold on to the hope that maybe he might understand to throw up in the pail. No such luck. Armed with another towel, I begin to prepare myself for sprinting. About thirty minutes after the initial episode (just as I'm finishing cleaning up the nastiness of the first) he begins to cry and wiggle around on the couch. This is my cue to get ready. He jumps down and begins to sprint around the house trying to run away from the discomfort, which he can't figure out is actually coming from inside of him. He wants to hide from his nausea, and man is he fast. I chase him around the house and try to steer him to an area that will be easier to clean until, finally, I catch him. To keep him there, my legs pin his legs down as we sit on the floor with him facing outward. The only reason I caught him was because he stopped, you guessed it, to puke. There is a limited amount of time to pin him down and get that towel up and ready. Then woosh - wam - projectile vomit. No, we couldn't just look down and puke. We have to launch vomit three feet in front of us! Sometimes the towel was up in time and sometimes not.

When we went through this the first time, it was NOT amusing. It wasn't until he was older and could finally use a trash can or toilet that I could look back and laugh about having to chase, pin, and raise the towel to play catch. Come on! Can't you laugh at the scene just described?

Snow

One year, when he was about three, we had a sizeable snowstorm. We bundled up and took our son outside for some snow fun. I had pictures in my head of building a snowman, throwing snowballs, and shoveling fun. Turns out he really didn't care for snow all that much. He looked at the snow, looked at me with the camera, and started to cry. Granted, the snow was up over his knees and he was bundled up like that kid in the movie, "A Christmas Story." So, maybe he had a right to cry. We tried to distract him by showing him how our dog loved to catch snowballs, and that worked for a short while. Then, out of frustration, he sits and throws himself on his back in the snow. Again, that kid from the movie! Laughing after snapping a picture, my husband and I take pity on him and bring him inside.

Never giving up on trying to get him to enjoy the snow more, one year our neighbor offered to tow him gently around the court with his quad. He sat on a large flat sled with a huge white helmet on his head going in circles. In our video, he looks like a little Storm Trooper. On that day, he didn't mind the snow so much.

Formal Picture Days

No matter the age, as most parents are, we were determined to have professional pictures taken of our son in the early years. Only one attempt was made to have his picture taken with Santa. This was during his second official Christmas. He was screaming his head off in the picture. The photo is one of my favorites, but the trauma of the whole experience was such that I just didn't have it in me to repeat the experience again the next Christmas. The trauma was for him - not for me. Dressed-up characters really freak him out, even as an older child. The staff at the Santa stop were upset because they couldn't get him to calm down and smile. I just laughed, shook my head, and told them to take the picture. It's a classic.

His fear and aversion of any person dressed up as a character continued for years. Even when we took him to Disney, he refused to stand anywhere near a character. That was all except for one incredible time. It was our last day there. We were waiting in line to board a Star Wars ride. Suddenly, Darth Vader approached! He walked by, then turned around and pointed at our son. I expected the usual panic, cringing, and hiding to happen. Instead, he marched right over to the guy, who was at least six feet tall and all in black and posed for a picture. (I guess Darth Vadar was way cooler than Santa Claus.)

Every year there would be an appointment at the local mall photography studio where we hoped to get just one good picture. The session always began as a challenge with tears and attempts to run away. But, then something amazing would happen. Our son would find a prop that he liked, and the photographer could get a few pictures. His favorite props were the car, truck, or fire engine. He would either stand next to it or sit in it or on it. Guaranteed, once he discovered it, we could get him to smile. He was pretty much bald his first few years, which made for some adorable pictures. I'm glad I made the effort to get him calm enough to take those shots and made the extra effort. Glassy-eyed from crying sitting in the truck, he has such a lovely mischievous smile.

As he got a little older, we progressed to the "preschool smile" - all teeth and more of a grimace. There are a few Christmas ornaments that he made in preschool with those pictures on them. I love them too, of course. However, we did wonder for a time if he would ever grow out of that toothy grimace!

Tantrums

When a full-blown tantrum starts at home over some small thing, it's interesting to take a step back and just watch. This distances you from the drama. Careful though, if your lips begin to twitch or a giggle slips out, watch out. Once they are old enough to understand, you will hear from them, "It's not funny!"

It's important to note that autistic meltdowns are not tantrums. There is a difference between having a sensory overload meltdown and a toddler tantrum. Our son would have both. Being able to tell the difference was fairly easy for me. But if you are not sure, ask yourself, "Is this an autistic meltdown due to sensory input overload from their surroundings or experiences or just a tantrum because they are not getting their way?"

Look For It

I hope the few examples that are given in this chapter make you smile. Humor can be found anywhere, and joy can be found in everyday life despite your difficulties. This may not come easily or naturally at first. For whatever reason, parts of our brains like to dwell on the negative. Actively choose to find joy and/or humor in a given situation. How you perceive things is your reality. You are in charge of it. Look for joy and laughter, and you will find it.

Chapter 11

Farewell For Now

So that's our story up to this point. I chose to stop here because our son's later journey through the public school years is different from this part of his life thus far. That will be book two. For now, I hope that our story of these early years has helped by giving you ideas, suggestions, recommendations, avenues to explore, and, most of all, hope.

Please know that although this path you are all taking together will be difficult at times, it still will be the most rewarding journey you will ever take. Each day working together you will all grow stronger and more confident. Love each other for who you are, not who you think the other person should be.

Life is a beautiful gift and so much more than just survival. Cherish the gift of life and each other despite your differences and difficulties. My wish for you all is that you thrive, not just survive!

References

American Academy of Family Physicians. "What Is Sensory Processing Disorder?" *Familydoctor.Org*, 20 Jan. 2022, familydoctor.org/condition/sensory-processing-disorder-spd.

"Asperger's Syndrome." *WebMD.com*, WebMD, LLC., 22 June 2022, https://www.webmd.com/brain/autism/ mental-health-aspergers-syndrome.

"Brush It Off! Brushing Protocol for Sensory Integration." *Play Works Therapy, Inc.*, 14 Apr. 2020, playworkschicago.co / brush-it-off-brushing-protocol-for-sensory-integration.

Clark, Christine. "Special Ed in Private Schools: What Parents Need to Know." *Commonwealth Learning Center*, http://www. commlearn.com/special-ed-in-private-schools-what-parents-need-to-know. Accessed 20 Jan. 2022.

"Early Intervention Services in New Jersey-Frequently Asked Questions." *NJ.Gov*, 29 Oct. 2015, www.nj.gov/ health/fhs/eis/documents/njeis_faq.pdf.

Groseclose, Kristen. "The Trouble with 'Welcome to Holland.' *S mithkingsmore.Org*, smithkingsmore.org/the trouble-with-welcome-to-holland. Accessed 22 Jan. 2022.

Heffron, Claire. "How a Sensory Diet Can Help Your Child: Guide and Resources." *Healthline*, Healthline Media, 8 Mar. 2019, www.healthline.com/health/guide-to-sensory-diet.

Hyman, M.D., FAAP, Susan L., et al., "Identification, Evaluation, and Management of Children With Autism Spectrum Disorder." *American Academy of Pediatrics*, vol. 145, no. 1, 2020, https://doi.org/10.1542/peds.2019-3447.

Iftikhar, M.D., Noreen. "Is It Safe to Give Kids Miralax for Constipation?" *Healthline*, Healthline Media a Red Ventures Company, 19 Feb. 2020, www.healthline.com/ health/childrens-health/miralax-for-kids.

"Jump and Crash! For Sensory Regulation." *Adapt & Learn*, 13 Aug. 2019, www.adaptandlearn.com/post/jump-crash-for-sensory-regulation.

Kingsley, Emily Perl. "Welcome to Holland." Copyright 1987. Reprinted with permission of the author.

"Learn the Signs of Autism." *Autismspeaks.Org*, www. autismspeaks.org/signs-autism. Accessed 20 Jan. 2022.

"Overview of Early Intervention." *Center for Parent Information & Resources*, U.S. Department of Education, 1 July 2021, www.parentcenterhub.org/ei-overview.

"Relationship Status among Parents of Children with Autism Spectrum Disorders: A Population-Based Study." *J Autism Dev Discord.*, vol. 42, no. 4, 2012, pp. 539–48. National Library of Medicine, pubmed.ncbi.nlm.nih.gov/21590433.

Sarris, Marina. "Under a Looking Glass: What's the Truth About Autism and Marriage." *Interactive Autism Network*, Kennedy Krieger Institute and Simons Foundation Partnership, 11 Apr. 2017, iancommunity.org/dev/whats-truth-about–autism- and-marriage.

"Signing Time - Teaching Sign Language." *Signing Time*, Two Little Hands Productions, signingtime.com. Accessed 20 Jan. 2022.

"Social Stories." *Raisingchildren.Net.Au,* Raising Children Network (Australia) Limited, raisingchildren.net.au/autism/therapies-guide/social-stories. Accessed 20 Jan. 2022.

"Solving Your Special Education Nightmare." *Complexchild.Org*, https://complexchild.org/articles/2012-articles/september/Solving-special-education-nightmare, Accessed 20 Jan. 2022.

"Swinging and Sensory Integration: How It Works." *Brain Balance,* Brain Balance Achievement Centers, www.brainbalancecenters.com/blog/swinging-sensory- integration-works#, Accessed 20 Jan. 2022.

"The Difference between IEPs and 504 Plans." *Understood,* Understood for All Inc., www.understood.org/en/articles/ the-difference-between-ieps-and-504-plans. Accessed 20 Jan. 2022.

"The Relative Risk And Timing of Divorce in Families of Children With An Autism Spectrum Disorder." *Journal of Family Psychology,* vol. 24, no. 4, 2010, pp. 449–57. National Library of Medicine, pubmed.ncbi.nlm.nih.gov/20731491.

"The Science of Greenspan Floor Time, Dr. Stanley Greenspan." *The Floortime Center,* thefloortimecenter.com/the- science-of-greenspan-floortime. Accessed 20 Jan. 2022.

"Your Child's Bedtime Routine." *Webmd.Com,* WebMD, LLC., 1 Dec. 2021, www.webmd.com/parenting/childs-bedtime#1.

"Your Child's Rights: Autism and School." *Autism Speaks,* www.autismspeaks.org/autism-school-your-childs-rights. Accessed 20 Jan. 2022.

Voyles Askham, Angie. "Brain Structure Changes in Autism, Explained." *Spectrum,* Simons Foundation, 15 Oct. 2020, www.spectrumnews.org/news/brain-structure-changes-in-autism-explained.

"What Are Joint Compressions?" *North Valley Pediatric Group*, nvpediatrictherapy.com/2020/10/27/what-are-joint-compressions. Accessed 20 Jan. 2022.

"What Is Applied Behavior Analysis?" *Autism Speaks*, www.autismspeaks.org/applied-behavior-analysis. Accessed 20 Jan. 2022.

"What Is 'Early Intervention'?" *Centers for Disease Control and Prevention*, www.cdc.gov/ncbddd/actearly/parents/states.html. Accessed 20 Jan. 2022.

"Why Is Routine so Important to People with ASD?" *Applied Behavior Analysis, EDU.Org*, www.appliedbehavioranalysis edu.org/hy-is-routine-so-important-to-people-with-asd. Accessed 20 Jan. 2022.

"What Is Speech Therapy?" *Autism Speaks*, www.autismspeaks.org/speech-therapy-autism. Accessed 20 Jan. 2022.